Dear Carol
Thank you &
friends to use an ins...

Happy Birthday 7/20/11

Shame on You

Rising From the Ashes of Shame To Face Guilt

By Shahrokh "Shah" Afshar

Shame on You: Shahrokh Afshar © 2011
Published by Vitreous Publishing

Photos on book jacket by: Michael Hevesey Photography
www.michaelhevesy.com

Graphic Designer: Wyce Ghiacy
www.visionfocusdesign.com
ISBN 978-0-9835422-3-0

Printed in Colombia

To my parents, Mansour and Hamdam, who formed me.

To my in-laws, Lyle and Gretchen McCart, who shaped me.

To my brothers, Shahram, Shahriar, and Shahdad, who loved me.

To my dear friend, Rich Buhler, who encouraged me.

Acknowledgement

A great thanks to my family, Karen, Todd, and Megan, and to Bob Hunt, Bob Barrett, Nate Mirza, Diana Richardson, Ray Driver, Michael Hevesy, Gianna Luisi, Susanne Wilson, Lisa Steele Hernandez and Michele Halverson who finished reading the draft just a few days before going to be with the Lord—I'll miss you. I am deeply indebted to all of you for helping me write this book.

Contents

A Personal Note

For years, my family, friends, and many who had heard me speak insisted that I write a book. And for years my reply was, "There are many good books already written by much better writers from my background. If anyone is interested, they can always read one of those books." However, I have come to realize as I get older that as a bicultural man who is quite fluent in two cultures, I do have much to offer both to Easterners and Westerners, Christians and non-Christians. That's why I finally sat down and wrote this book.

MAY 24, 1969

It's two in the morning. My plane just landed in Los Angeles International Airport. I'm not quite 19, have never been this far away from my family, don't know anyone, can barely say anything in English, and my only contact information is the address to an ESL language school.

No sooner do I get off the plane than I experience my first disappointment in the United States. The blond hair, blue-eyed bombshell isn't waiting to pick me up in her convertible. I don't know how she's supposed to know I was coming, but that's what usually took place in Annette Funicello and Frankie Avalon's Hollywood beach party movies that I had seen in Iran.

I give the address to a cab driver and get in the back of the car. Forty minutes later we are in front of a locked-down language school in downtown LA. The cab driver gets out of his taxi and bangs on the doors, but we both know nobody's there. He then suggests that I check into the hotel across the street.

I never knew how many people of different races lived in America. The hotel lobby is full of them, most of whom I later find to be pimps, hookers, and drug addicts. This is my first encounter with the real America.

The next morning I put on my suit and tie, cross the street, and register at the ESL school. This is my first day in America.

1

My parents are first cousins. According to my mom, Hamdam (no, the name has nothing to do with pork or damnation; literally it means "the one who shares even her breath with you, a comforter"), at the time of her birth, her umbilical cord was cut in my dad's name. In other words, at her birth, my mom was appointed to become Mansour's future wife. At the time my dad was 10 years old. I guess you could call that the ultimate arranged marriage. They got married when she turned 15, and she had me a year later. I'm the oldest of four boys.

Like the other 90% of Abadanis (people from Abadan), my parents had migrated to that city. Soon after they married in the late '40s, my dad felt the oil company in Abadan offered him a great future, so they moved there. They were originally from Fars, a province in the south central region of Iran, the location of Takht-e Jamshid (Persepolis)—the ceremonial capital of the Persian Empire during the Achaemenid dynasty where Cyrus, one of the greatest kings in history, is buried.

They brought with them my mom's much younger sister, Parichehr, and a young farmer, Fazl-ullah, who lived in my grandfather's villages. Eventually Parichehr became like our oldest sister. My parents found Fazl-ullah a wife, Sahab, and their son, Bahram, became like one of my brothers. Fazl-ullah passed away in the '80s, and Bahram got married and eventually moved out; but Sahab, my second mother, still lives with my parents.

2

I was born in Abadan, the most beautiful city in the world, or at least it used to be. It's located in the province of Khuzestan in southwestern Iran on Abadan Island. It is in the delta of Aravand Roud, (Farsi for "Majesty" or "Grandeur River") or Shatt al-Arab (Arabic for "Arabs' River") at the head of the Persian Gulf, which carries the waters of the two very biblical rivers, the Euphrates and the Tigris Rivers. We just called it "Shatt." The

southern end of the river establishes the border between Iraq and Iran down to the mouth of the river as it discharges into the Persian Gulf. In those days Abadan, an important oil refining and shipping center in the world, was the last stop of many major oil pipelines.

My city was an unimportant village until the discovery of nearby oil fields in 1908. In 1910 the population of Abadan was around 400. Its oil refinery, which was commissioned in 1913 and built by the Anglo-Persian Oil Company, was the largest in the world by the '70s. Sanat-eh Naft-eh Abadan (Oil Company of Abadan) necessitated a vast number of employees—more than 220,000 people in 1956, most who had migrated from almost every part of the nation. This made Abadanis quite unique and different than the rest of the Iranians. Like America, except for some natives, the majority of the people of Abadan had migrated from other parts of the country.

My birthplace was where the West met the East. Away from family, friends, and cultural peer pressure, Abadanis were much more open to new things and changes than the rest of the nation.

At least in our neighborhoods, we had a decent mixture of shame-based and guilt-based cultures living side by side. We lived in an environment of honor that stemmed out of *keeping* the law. This was quite unusual in that part of the world where, for the most part, the only law is whatever brings you honor and keeps shame away.

I believe what set Abadan apart from the rest of the country was the fact that it was populated by displaced people who were more open to change. The great church historian, Latourette, might not be too far off the mark when referring to the first century Italians who had moved to Carthage on the heels of the Roman conquest:

> Uprooted from their Italian environment, traditional Italian customs and religions may have had less hold on the immigrants and their children than in Italy and there may have been greater open-mindedness to the Christian message.[1]

Unfortunately, the refinery, together with much of the city, was destroyed during the Iran-Iraq war in the '80s. Although the Iranian government has made some attempt to rebuild the city, she will never be the same. What made the city great were not her buildings, streets, or the oil refinery, but a spirit that is no longer there.

3

My mother ran the household with an iron fist. Contrary to the popular Western belief, although Middle Eastern culture might appear male-dominant, that's not so—at least not behind closed doors at home. My mom did all the cooking, cleaning, shopping, and managing the household finances. She was the brain behind much of my dad's financial decision-making. When you consider how the simple act of grocery shopping took almost all day, then add to that four active boys, my aunt, and Fazl-ullah and his family, my mom had her hands full—but that did not stop her from having fun in life.

Often in the afternoons, a few hours before the men came home from work, the neighborhood women got together to cook a huge pot of *Aash-eh Reshteh*, a traditional Iranian noodle soup. Once the *Aash*, as we called it, was prepared, all of us kids sat on the floor around a traditional tablecloth called *sof-reh* with a huge pot of hot *Aash* placed in the middle of it and fought over who was going to have the first bowl. Unlike Westerners, we didn't eat dinner till around eight in the evening. The *Aash* was supposed to tie us over till then.

One afternoon, in my haste to get the first bowl, as I reached for the ladle submerged deep in a hot pot of soup, I hit the handle so hard that some of the soup catapulted into my friend's face. Though he screamed in agony for a while, once he quieted down, thankfully, we could tell that he wasn't hurt much.

Lifelong friendships were built around those *sof-rehs* and hot, delicious bowls of *Aash*. Even today I consider breaking bread with others a sacred act and one of the most effective ways of establishing relationships.

4

I have three younger brothers. Just like mine, their names start with the title "shah," which means king. Before our births, my parents had placed the names they'd chosen for their children in different parts of the family Quran. Upon our births, my dad randomly opened the family Quran, and the first name he came across was designated to the newborn.

These are old traditional Persian names and not the common Arabic/Muslim names. My name, Shahrokh, means "face of the king." My second brother, Shahram (king's loyal subject), is eighteen months younger than I; and Shahriar (friend or supporter of the king), the third one, was born eighteen months after Shahram. My youngest brother, Shahdad (gift of the king), who is affectionately called Tah-towghari, literally "the bottom of the pot," is eight years younger than I.

If you think you have a hard time pronouncing the names, you should've heard my angry mom trying to call out our names when we were in the middle of a fight. All you could hear was, "Ssssssssssssssh…." I'm just grateful our mother didn't know how to swear in English.

19

One of my greatest regrets in life is not getting to know or spend more time with my brothers when I was younger. When I left Iran, Shahram was 17, Shahriar was 15, and Shahdad, whom I didn't get to know at all, was only 11. I was the typical older brother—a jerk who was too cool to hang out with his younger siblings, and then I was separated from them for a long time. My three brothers have a much closer relationship than I do with my parents and each other.

5

As we were growing up, my dad had a great relationship with us boys. Much of who I am today is directly related to the man God allowed to be my earthly *baba*, as we call our fathers in Farsi. The following stories will give the readers a better picture of the greatest father any man could have.

My dad has a great sense of humor. Even in his late 80s, he still lights up any gathering with his presence, stories, and jokes. He's also notorious for taking a joke you just told him, changing the names and parts of the set up, and telling the joke right back to you. To a certain degree my brothers and I have inherited that sense of humor and take a great joy in making those around us laugh at our jokes.

It was our *baba* who taught us how to "pants" each other, which in turn we did to him. This tradition I've proudly passed on to my son, Todd, who, even today at the age of 27, would happily do it to his dad whenever he gets the chance. Like my dad, I've tried to be a good father and a close friend to my children.

While my dad's taking a shower, Shahriar, Shahram, and I hide under his bed in his bedroom. He's got no idea we're there. As soon as he enters the room, he drops the towel that's wrapped around him, so he can dress. We are shaking uncontrollably because we want to laugh out loud, but can't.

21

Holding back, I guess Shahriar is building up way too much pressure in his intestines, which forces him to let out a loud fart. Well, you can imagine what happens next. We can't control ourselves any longer and start to laugh hysterically trying to get out from under the bed. My dad chases us out of the room screaming, "Pedar sag-ha" (literally "children whose father is a dog," a phrase that's often used in an endearing way), trying to cover his front with the towel and his behind with the other hand.

6

ven as a child I was interested in religion. At the age of seven during the month of Ramadan, or Ramezan as we called it, like most Muslims, I tried to do the ritual fast. This was where from sunrise to sunset a Muslim is supposed to abstain from eating, drinking, or anything else that might bring him pleasure. In my case the fast only lasted for a couple of hours, and I never tried it again until years later. I got way too hungry.

My parents have been to Mecca. My mother is a very religious and God–fearing Muslim woman, but not fanatical. Every year, in honor of the martyred saints of the Shias—the Prophet's grandchildren, Hassan and Hussein, she had a *Sof-reh-eh Nazr* at our house.

A group of my mom's invited friends sat around a huge *sof-reh* that was spread on the carpeted floor, where they ate traditional *halva* (an especially sweet pastry made for this occasion), nuts, fruit, and candy and listened to a wailing *Aakhond* (a Shia clergyman) reciting, blow-by-blow, the historical event of the two grandchildren being slaughtered by their enemies. The object of the recitation was to whip the ladies into a frenzy of tears and chest beating. Somehow, it's believed, the harder one weeps and beats herself, the more she's in a place of having her wish granted.

However, what shaped my life wasn't so much my religious upbringing as much as it was my parents, our shame-based culture, and Abadan's unique culture.

It's a summer day. My mom is having one of her annual Sof-rehs in the guestroom. There's going to be a match at the neighborhood swimming pool; but to my extreme sorrow, I can't participate. I'm very sick and lying on the bed sulking when my uncle Sia walks into the room. In his hand he's holding a wrapped candy taken from the Sof-reh.

"How're you feeling?" he asks.

"Not good. I wish I was at the pool."

I don't remember how the subject gets there, but he says, "If you believe, eating this candy can heal you."

I believe and eat the candy. Within half an hour I'm standing in front of the pool talking to my friends with no sign of the illness.

Who or what healed me? Was the healing psychosomatic? Was it the sanctified candy from a Muslim ritual that healed me? Was it Allah, Khoda (the Zoroastrian supreme being, a name Persians use for God), or God?

7

Abadanis spoke, dressed, and ate differently. When visiting other cities, wearing our Lee jeans and jackets and speaking the Abadani language—a mixture of Farsi, Arabic, and English that I like to call *Farbglish*, people immediately knew we were from Abadan.

Many Iranian comedians from other parts of the country made fun of our accent, language, and how we loved to exaggerate. After 40 years of living in the U.S., many older Iranians can still tell I'm from the south because of my Abadani accent. Some Abadanis invented a new language, which consisted of pronouncing the words backward. That drove any outsider up the wall. We even had our own music genre called Bandari, or the music of the shores.

The city was divided into two sections. The local government had developed the downtown area, but the majority of the city was designed and built by the oil company's Western planners. Any outsider could immediately recognize the difference between the part of the city developed by the local government and the section designed by the oil company.

With her brick track housing, front yards, manicured evergreen hedges dividing each house, and paved roads lined with palm trees, the city developers had patterned Abadan after a Western resort city.

At the time when the rest of the country (even downtown Abadan) still used outhouses, we enjoyed indoor plumbing and a complete sewer system. I'd never used a public bath till my first trip out of Abadan. We had rotary phones, whereas the rest of the country, except in the capital, either didn't have phones or used the crank kind. Abadan was the most unique city in Iran.

Abadanis were also legendary for their gifts of hospitality and unparalleled faithfulness to friends—two qualities that are still very close to my heart. Iranians from other parts of the country used to say, "When in Abadan you're not allowed to put your hand in your pocket." This meant that as long as you're hanging out with your Abadani host, you're not allowed to spend any of your own money.

In any traditional Iranian house, the guestroom or formal living room is the most important part of the house. With great exceptions, the room is supposed to be used only when you have guests. Under lock and key, it's often stocked with the best silverware, china, pastry, fruit, drinks, and mixed nuts. None of us children were supposed to go near all those goodies, but we'd often raid the closet where they were kept. My mom kept the key to the closet under the Persian carpet covering the tile floor of the living room, and all the boys knew it.

Those days it was quite common for guests, even from far away, to arrive at our house unannounced. If what we had to offer them wasn't worthy of a guest, as the guests walked in the front door, it was not unusual for my mother to send me out the back door to ask our next door neighbor for some fruits, nuts, or sweets to offer our newly arrived guest. In that culture, not to offer your guest the best of all you could afford was considered to be a great insult.

In September 1980 when Iraqi forces took over the neighboring city of Khorramshahr, Abadan was besieged for 18 months. Although extremely unequipped, Abadanis took up arms and defended their city themselves; consequently, she was never captured.

It's one hot afternoon on a summer day. My buddy and I are meeting up at his house to go to the neighborhood pool. Before I walk out of the house, I do a taboo. I take a huge Lebanese apple out of the refrigerator and sneak out. I'm safe. My mom doesn't catch me take something that's reserved only for guests.

As I get on the street and take my first bite into that sweet gift from God, I come face to face with Mr. Torabi, the local grocery shop owner. He immediately knows why I'm sneaking out of the house; my mother purchased those expensive apples from him for guests—not for her son.

"La mazhab (infidel), YOU shouldn't be eating that expensive apple," he yells at me.

Amazed at his intuition, I let out a nervous laugh and walk away hoping he'll not report me to my mother the next time she goes shopping.

8

In a Western culture, to break the law makes one guilty. Most people of such a society do their best to stay on the right side of the law, so they won't be found guilty. A culture that operates on these premises is called a guilt-based culture.

A large majority of third-world nations are dominated by what's called a shame-based culture. The action most revered in such a culture is that which brings him, his family, and his community honor and not shame. Often one might go as far as cheating, lying, stealing, and even killing to keep his honor. That's the culture I was raised in and which influenced me during my formative years.

Under the shame-based culture, attaining a higher education is one way to gain honor in the community. Every parent longs to introduce his child as "my daughter the physician" or "my son the engineer."

Sending your kids to college after high school is almost a mandate for any Iranian family that can afford it. That's why Iranians living in the U.S. are the third most educated minority group in the nation.

I'm grateful that my parents were different. None of us brothers were ever forced to become this or that because they wished us to be so, but this isn't to say we're immune from a culture that tied a person's respectability to the level of his education. From childhood almost every one of the Afshar boys knew what we wanted to be when we grew up.

We lived to gain honor for the family and, at all costs, to avoid any appearance of shame.

———————————————————————

I'm visiting my parents who're staying with my brother Shahdad in Northern California. This is their second visit to the U.S. As I walk into the living room, I witnessed some of the most fascinating conversations I've ever heard.

My parents are watching that bastion of American morality, Jerry Springer. My mom doesn't speak English, so she's relying on my dad's translation.

"So what's happening, Afshar?" (It's common for Iranian wives to call their husbands by their last names.)

My dad clears his throat and says, "Hmmm, this guy's married to the fat woman on the left, but he's also been having sex with the younger woman on the right who's the fat woman's daughter from her fourth marriage."

"What? They're talking about all this stuff on TV?" my mom replies with a raised voice. She then begins to smack herself on her head—a gesture used in time of mourning or extreme distress and shame—repeatedly saying, "Khaak baar saraam" (literally "dirt on my head," a phrase used when one feels deeply ashamed).

To most decent people, it's appalling that a man would commit such a heinous act of sleeping with his stepdaughter; but to my mother, as an Iranian raised in a shame-based culture, an even greater transgression is openly announcing the ungodly act to the whole world and celebrating it. The lack of regard for one's honor is an unforgivable behavior.

You'd think after such a shock, one would stop watching the show, but not my mom.

"What else, Afshar? What else? Tell me, tell me," she badgers my dad.

9

I love my three brothers. Shahram has a heart bigger than the whole world. He's got this incredible gift of staying in touch with all his family members and friends. Up to this day, he knows in what part of the world most of his classmates live and how to contact them—he knows the majority of the phone numbers by heart. But above all, he loves to laugh and make others do the same.

During an inter-neighborhoods' swimming competition, right after the heats were over and before the water polo match, out of nowhere and completely unannounced, Shahram provided the crowd with much laughter by jumping off the diving board dressed in my dad's suit jacket. Unfortunately, after he had left his brand new pants on the chain-link fence to dry, a visiting outsider stole them, something that my mom never let him forget.

When it comes to throwing rocks, Shahram and I are a great team. We both have deadly aims, so the kid standing 50–60 feet away is no match for us. As he is walking away and mouthing at us, Shahram and I each pick up a rock and throw them at him. As he dodges one rock, he runs smack into another one. His head is cracked open. We run home leaving the kid by himself. The next day we see him. He's OK. The wound is superficial. He'll live.

10

The oil company promoted a strong sense of community. We had our own local schools. Most students grew up in the same neighborhood. Our parents were close friends who were also, mostly, co-workers.

We lived in an L-shaped five-room and one bathroom house in an area called Segosh-eh Braim (literally, "the triangle of Braim"). Four of the rooms were clustered together on one side of the house. We had two bedrooms—my parent's room and ours, the boys. Then, there were the dining room and the formal living room, which served as the guest room.

There was a square concrete courtyard separating the kitchen and the adjacent servant's room—the fifth—from the rest of the house. The four rooms on one side and a six or seven foot L-shaped brick wall on the other side surrounded the courtyard. On the far corner of the courtyard there was an outhouse, which, unlike the rest of the country, was not just a hole in the ground that one squatted over, but equipped with running water, underground sewage, and a Middle Eastern porcelain toilet with an overhead flush tank. Beyond the courtyard, outside the house, was our beloved vegetable garden, which we all adored.

Neighborhoods had their own clubs with huge ballrooms where we danced the latest Western dance styles and heard popular singers in concert. We had a golf club—I used to caddy for my dad—a polo club, a boat club, and a few other clubs. The neighborhood stores were stocked with imported goods from all over Europe.

Our movie theaters showed some of the most recent Hollywood releases in English. My brothers and I watched the movies with much interest; although, not speaking any English, we had no idea what the plots were all about. After we saw the movie *Bullet*, all we did was to make a wavy gesture with our hands and say, "San Francisco, you know!"

Being highly influenced by the Western culture along with most of my friends, I grew up listening to Western pop music. I loved the groups like The Beatles, Dave Clark 5, and Jefferson Airplane; but my favorite was Eric Burden and The Animals. I used to carry a photo of the band in my wallet.

As I'm writing this in San Fernando, California, I'm listening to the *Best of the Animals*, laughing at how little I understood the lyrics as a teenager. Who knew that the song "House of the Rising Sun" was about a house of prostitution?

But my greatest joy was our neighborhood swimming pools. They were the envy of the rest of the country. It was in those pools that some of the best swimmers in the nation rose to prominence.

11

On four separate occasions, my aunt could have killed me. Parichehr, who is seven years older than I, grew up as our older sister.

When I was a newborn, she took me for a walk in my huge British pram with its large wheels. After a while she must have gotten tired of walking with me, so she decided to push the pram as hard as she could and chase after it. Well, in her second or third attempt, the baby carriage hit a bump on the sidewalk and flipped over on top of me. For some reason I received no injuries.

A few months later, when I was only a year or so old, she fed me an entire Bundt cake with walnuts in it. I ended up with terrible constipation, which landed me in ER. My dad tells a funny story about how he got me to the hospital.

At the time he didn't have a car, so he caught a cab. As he comes out of the traffic circle and gets to the front of the emergency entrance, he tells the driver to stop the car, but the man continues driving.

My dad shouts, "*Man, stop the car!*"

"I can't," replies the driver very sheepishly.

"*Why not?*"

"Because my cab doesn't have any brakes."

After going around the traffic circle for the second time, the cab finally came to a stop and my dad was able to get out with me in his arms. The doctor suggested an enema, which in those days was applied with an aspirator. Once again my dad had to raise his voice, but this time he was yelling at the male nurse who was about to perform the procedure on me with an adult-size aspirator.

"Do you think your grown-up ass could handle such a large tube? If not, then what makes you think this little boy could handle an aspirator that size?"

I'm so glad my dad intervened and a baby-size aspirator was eventually used.

You'd think after the second attempt on my life, my parents weren't going to put their oldest son in Parichehr's care once again; but no, the saga continued.

Just a few months later, in the middle of a hot summer day, she locked me up in a car for quite a while. Thank God my parents rescued me before I died of a heatstroke.

On her last attempt to kill me, when I was only five, after teasing me, Parichehr ran away and jumped on the swing in our front yard. As she was swinging back and forth, I picked up a stick and tried to hit her. Misjudging the speed of the swing, I charged as she came towards me; and before I knew it, I was hit in the face, flew for about six or seven feet, and landed on a small tree behind me. Needless to say, I was rushed to the emergency again. This time I spent a few days in the hospital with a concussion.

I often wonder if my lack of ability to remember names, numbers, directions, and other things has something to do with, thanks to Parichehr, how many times I was hit in the head when I was a child.

12

loved hanging out with my dad. He was a great teacher, but I mostly learned by watching him.

One night he and I were at the theater when he received an urgent call. He took me with him to his office, which was located at the main gate of the refinery. His officers had arrested a young black Arab burglar for breaking and entering. My dad knew the man. It wasn't the first time he had been arrested. He took the young man aside, talked to him for a while, and then gave him some money and let him go. His act of kindness has been forever ingrained upon my heart.

On hot summer days I rode my bike to deliver my dad's lunch, along with a bottle of watermelon juice freshly juiced by my mother. His office was a good six to eight miles away from our house, but I looked forward to this job.

After delivering my dad's lunch, I'd get to sit in his office, play with different instruments, color, write, and watch him interact with co-workers and other employees. After hanging out in my dad's office for a while, it became clear to me that Iranian employees treated each other differently than the way they treated the Westerners. Iranians respected the foreigners more, but why?

I'm tired of sitting in my dad's office, so I go out and stand at the main gate. There are two guards standing at each side of the gate checking the incoming and outgoing cars, trucks, and laborers. They check inside and under each vehicle to make sure nobody is stealing anything. Some of the pedestrians are even frisked before they're allowed to leave the premises. Suddenly a motorcycle with a sidecar appears. The rider is an American. He's waved through. Without slowing down, he zips right through the gate waving at the guards. I'm left puzzled.

Later I relay the incident to my dad and ask the following, "Baba, how come all the Iranians were searched before leaving but not the American?"

There's a twinkle in his eyes.

He takes me to the next office where his Assyrian superior, Mr. Badal, is sitting and asks me to repeat the question. So I do.

They both look at each other and smile. I know I've asked an insightful question but don't know why it's so. I can also tell my dad's proud of me, and that means the whole world to me, but neither one answers my question.

Even at this young age, by his reaction, my dad is teaching me not to be afraid to ask tough questions. It'll be awhile before these questions are answered.

13

o you remember your first day of kindergarten? For most, it was the first time you'd been separated from your parents. Some kids were running around with snot dripping down to their lips, crying because they were scared, missing their parents. Your name and address were written on a piece of paper which was pinned to your shirt; and like a UPS parcel, you were ready to be shipped to some exotic place. All you were missing was the universal barcode on your forehead. "Make sure you get on bus 53 on the way home," the teachers instructed you.

I liked kindergarten because my nature has always craved fellowship and making new friends. In Abadan friends were made for life; and that's how, up to this day, I view friendship: not as something out of convenience and for the moment, but something for life even through hardships.

We were at school for only half a day; during that time we got to learn new things and play like crazy. My favorite activity was sliding down a mammoth slide—at least it appeared so to a five-year-old. This was done only once or twice a year. My God, that was a great ordeal.

First, all the several hundred students had to line up by class. After waiting what seemed to be a lifetime, you were sent to the bottom of the steps where a teacher was waiting to send you up to the teacher on the top of the slide; and eventually the third teacher caught you at the bottom of the slide. The waiting and the anticipation alone were intense enough to make some students wet their pants; but once you began the journey down hill, it was worth all the wet pants in the world.

My dad and I are driving by the water purification plant.

I ask, "Baba, where does rain come from?"

Pointing at the steam coming out of the smokestacks, he says, "From the steam."

I am sure he explained it better than that, but that's all I understood.

The very next day, when my kindergarten teacher asks, "Who knows where rain comes from?" I quickly raise my hand.

"Yes, Shahrokh?"

"Steam, Mrs. Teacher," I shout.

My teacher is beside herself. "How in heaven's name would a five-year-old know anything about rain?" she asks herself.

In the next several hours my teacher keeps bringing other teachers to the class and has me answer the same question over and over again. By the end of the day, the school principal gives me an award. That's the only time in my life that I received an award for anything closely resembling an academic achievement. I love kindergarten.

14

My parents never spanked me. But I'm certain that at times they wanted to kill me.

One summer day when I was only six years old, my dad bought me a lottery ticket. The next day I found out that I'd won five *tu-mans* (the Iranian currency), which at the time was worth less than a dollar.

Without telling my parents, I took my five *tu-mans* and treated a friend to the movies. We took a bus and then a cab to get to the theater. On the way back, having run out of money, we took the bus all the way home. By the time I got home it was after 11 in the evening. My parents, along with some of the neighbors and a policeman, thinking the worst, were waiting for me. To the best of my recollection, that was the only time that my dad chased me around the front yard with a stick planning my funeral, but thank God the neighbors stopped him.

15

In most Muslim nations, schools are segregated by gender, and the first grade starts at the age of seven. However, the private school we went to was coed, and my parents worked it out so I started the first grade when I turned six.

The Iranian school system was based mostly on memorization, and I have a very poor memory. So, academically I always sucked at school. However, for several reasons, throughout school I was always popular. Being a natural-born leader, a faithful friend, good at sports, a great storyteller, and loving the underdog, kids liked me.

I often was picked to be a team captain. In second grade, one of my classmates, Arzhang, was a handicapped boy. From what I remember, he had very weak muscles, and, to run, he had to literally swing his legs to his side and throw them one at a time in front of him.

When it came to picking teammates, Arzhang was the first person I chose. I knew we were going to lose the relay due to his handicap; but I also knew if I didn't pick him, no one else would, or he'd be the last to get picked. Winning was not as important to me as much as making sure my friend was taken care of. He also could kick pretty hard and straight when it came to playing soccer.

I may have had a poor memory when it came to memorizing my time-tables, but I was one of those kids who, after seeing a movie once, could remember every scene, action by action, and every dialogue, word by word. This was especially so when the movie was in English and, along with my friends, I had no idea what the plot was all about. I made up my own stories, which were probably much more interesting than the actual plot. That, in addition to books I read every summer, made me the class storyteller. When a teacher was late to the class, by popular demand, I entertained the students till she showed up.

16

Shahriar, my second brother, is an extremely successful pharmacist and lives in the States with his family. He's always a step ahead of what the popular trend in medicine might be. His pharmacy is one of the best in the city and has won several awards for customer support and service. According to him, he's built his whole business on one principle we all learned from our parents: relationship, relationship, and relationship.

In high school he was a holy terror, making my dad show up at the principal's office often to explain, for example, why his son had drawn a nude sketch of his math teacher that was passed around in the class.

One day after school's morning session when all the students went home for lunch, he walked up to tell me that one of the older kids had punched him earlier. As we were walking through a field adjacent to our school, 25th of Shahrivar, I told him, "Shari, pick up the largest rock you can find, sneak up to the kid that punched you, hit him as hard as you can, and then run back toward me." This must have been one of the few times that Shahriar actually listened to me and did exactly what I told him.

The kid was one of the tallest boys at school; he eventually played on the Iranian national basketball team. Shahriar hit him so hard that he almost jumped out of his shoes. Immediately he turned around to attack my brother, who was running back towards me. And now it was my turn to charge the kid. He knew he was no match for my friends and me, so he took off in the opposite direction never to bother Shahriar again.

Eventually he became a good friend of my brothers, but he never let Shahriar forget that he could have been a much better basketball player if Shahriar had not hit him so hard.

17

I**'ve always been quick to want to take people's pains away and solve their problems.** Part of it has to do with the way my parents raised me, but I believe much of it is due to the way God created me. I've always cared for people more than an average person would.

In third grade I was chosen to be the school's band conductor. Don't ask me why. I have no musical talent. At a very young age I could sing, but as soon as I hit puberty, I began to sound like Frankenstein screaming at the sight of fire. I guess Mr. Shoora, the music teacher, happened to like the way I moved the baton.

In fourth grade our school band was given the great privilege of performing before the Shah of Iran, Reza Pahlavi, who was visiting Abadan. In preparation for that occasion, we had to practice in Abadan's great theater, Cinema Taj.

Our main soloist had just lost her father in a tragic car accident. She was quite distraught. Under any other circumstance, she would not have been there, but this was a once in a lifetime opportunity.

As the band began to rehearse, she stepped up to the mike to sing. She only managed to sing the first couple of bars before, like a soldier under fire looking for cover, she abruptly turned around and rushed towards the back of the stage. She didn't make it very far and threw up right on the stage.

To my amazement and utter sadness, all the kids were disgusted with what took place. As if the poor girl had done it deliberately! Up to this day I don't understand why none of the adults did anything to comfort my friend. I was the only one who walked up, put my arms around her, and, with the best a ten year old could, tried to comfort her by saying, "It's going to be OK!"

A week later we performed before Reza Shah. What a great privilege that was! The next day I came down with the mumps and missed school for the following month.

I'm only five sitting at the foot of the bed crying.

"Why are you crying, Shahrokh jan," My dad asks compassionately.

"Do you remember last night coming out of Cinema Taj?" I ask.

"Of course, I do. But why are you crying?"

"You didn't give any money to the beggar sitting against the wall begging for money."

18

I **loved summertime in Abadan.** For about seven months out of the year, the weather was quite uncomfortable there, but from the end of June to the middle of September the heat was unbearable. The temperature was constantly in triple digits. For that reason the schools in Abadan went on summer vacation a few weeks earlier than the rest of the country. With an outside temperature over 100 degrees, having to sit in classrooms with no air-conditioning was plain uncomfortable and at times even deadly. It was not unusual for Abadanis to die of heatstroke during the summer. I took pride in the fact that often our city was the hottest place in the nation.

In our house we had two A/C wall units, which were placed in the guestroom and the boy's bedroom room. So inside the house we were very much protected from the heat, but on the outside it was a different story. Our activities were limited to either nighttime basketball or my great love, swimming.

Like all of our friends, my brothers and I knew how to swim well. We spent our whole summer literally living in the neighborhood pool, which opened at 8 a.m., closed at noon for lunch, opened again at 1 p.m., and stayed open till 10 p.m.

Except for Tuesdays and Thursdays, which from 8 to 10 in the morning were ladies' days, we were usually at the pool by 9 a.m. After swimming for three hours, we went home for lunch and a quick nap. Around 3 p.m. we were back again. We swam till 6 p.m., went home to get something to eat, then came back again to swim till 10 p.m. Even though every other year my dad got almost three months of vacation in summertime, we hardly ever went anywhere. No other place in Iran could offer us a more enjoyable summer than Abadan.

Nobody used goggles or put on sunscreen lotion while swimming. By noon, due to the chlorine—up to this day still my favorite smell—our eyes hurt so much we could barely keep them open; and our very dark skin was so dry, we could actually etch our names on our arms.

On the way home we pulled our wet trunks over our heads to keep them cool; then we closed our eyes, put our hands on each other's shoulders like the three blind mice, and followed the designated guide—who, with *his* eyes open, walked us home. Sometimes we would take off our sandals and dare each other to see who could walk the farthest on the heat-stricken, melting, and bubbling asphalt. Living in Abadan was one of the greatest privileges I've experienced in my life.

At the beginning of every summer, my parents purchased enough watermelons to fill a small pickup truck, which lasted us for most of the summer. We stored them in front of the air-conditioning unit in the guestroom. Up to this day it's still a mystery to me how the melons lasted that long and never went bad.

Once we got home after swimming all morning, the four of us split two watermelons, and each one of us ate a half. This was supposed to tide us over till my father came home for lunch. During the summer, due to the heat, the oil company employees went to work early when it was still relatively cool and worked till 2 in the afternoon. While waiting for my dad to come home for lunch, I read. I read scores of books during those hot summer days. By the time I reached high school, I'd read many of the classics such as *Les Miserable, Robinson Crusoe,* and *Brothers Karamazov*; but my favorites were Mickey Spillane's Mike Hammer books.

In Abadan, like in the rest of the country, there were concrete drainage ditches along the streets between the curbs and the sidewalks. In the summertime these ditches were full of tiny fish and, at times, infested with frogs. All of the neighborhood kids paired up, straddling on each side of the ditch; we'd approach each other from the opposite side trying to trap and catch the fish with our hands. But as we got older, it was more fun to shoot the frogs in the ditches with our BB guns.

There's nothing more I miss about Iran than those summer days in Abadan. Unfortunately, we all know that the past can never be recreated.

19

My dad taught me how to swim, but my mom instigated it. Only five years old, one summer day I was swimming in what we called the "children's pool" along with other kids my age. This wading pool was shallow, and the water didn't come any higher than my little knees. Standing knee-high in water, minding my own business, and moving my arms as if I was swimming the free style, I heard my mother calling me. Apparently pretend swim was not good enough for my parents, so they'd come up with their own scheme.

"Your dad wants to talk to you," she told me and proceeded to pull me out of the pool. She walked me to the shallow side of the big pool where my dad was waiting for me. "What do you want dad?" I asked. As if he couldn't hear me, he motioned to me to get closer. As I got to the edge of the pool—yes, you can guess what happened, my mom pushed me in.

I remember going up and down a few times before my dad finally grabbed me, but I don't remember anything after that. However, what I do remember is that, from that day on, I never went back to the children's pool; except when a group of us older kids, with no grownups around, would try to see who could belly dive in the shallow pool without scraping his face on the bottom of the pool.

Unwittingly my parents taught me a great lesson on leadership training: throw your student in the pool and only help him if he asks for it; otherwise, stay out of his way and let him figure it out on his own—no micromanaging. My dad knew I had the potential to become a good swimmer. All I needed was a push from my mom. By the way, he was correct!

20

Shahdad is my youngest brother. He's an outstanding family man. He and his wife are one of those typical American couples who graciously spend more time living in their SUV bussing their kids to soccer, water polo, and swimming events than living at home. He is also a successful radiologist in Northern California.

Soon after Shahdad was born, the doctor determined that he was lactose intolerant and had to drink goat's milk. My parents did something very unusual in our neighborhood—they purchased a goat so Shahdad could drink its milk. Almost all the neighbors had chicken coops where they raised chickens and turkeys, but nobody had goats.

Because of Shahdad's condition, we got used to having livestock at our house. So years later when a friend offered my parents a lamb, we jumped on the opportunity and accepted the offer. We treated the creature, the lamb, like our pet, and called him Koochool. We taught him how to charge and butt people. Having him around was so much fun.

We used to throw one of us in the courtyard with Koochool. Then locking all the doors and giving the person no access to the inside of the house, we had a great time laughing at him or her running around the courtyard trying to avoid being butted.

Our backyard gate is made out of a one-fourth-inch thick sheet metal. I've been teasing the lamb for a while getting him to charge me. With his head down as Koochool backs off to charge me, I turn around to run away from him. Forgetting that I've left the gate only partially open, I run smack into the metal gate and split my forehead open. As I'm sitting on the ground in a daze, bleeding profusely with Koochool attacking me, my mother who is watching us through the bathroom window is laughing her head off. I guess raising four sons and watching us go through an array of injuries, she finds this incident quite amusing. I still have a half-inch scar in the middle of my forehead as a reminder not to ever mess with horned animals.

21

y brothers and I weren't mean-spirited, but we were mischievous. Every Thursday night during the summer, we went to *Bashgah-e-Naft* (the Oil Club) to catch a movie at an outdoor theater. The club was not very far from our home, so after the movie a group of us kids walked home. A mile from our home, there was always a Volkswagen Beatle parked in front of a house. On several occasions, we all lifted and carried the "Bug" over the drainage ditch and placed it on the sidewalk. I still wonder how the man was able to get his car on the street the following day.

On very rare summer days when we had nothing to do, the Afshar brothers had a slingshot war. These slingshots were made out of hairpins and rubber bands. You might laugh, but by using small U-shaped pieces of chain-link fence as ammo, these little slingshots could blind a person.

Two of us took our positions behind some furniture in the guestroom and the other two hid in the boys' bedroom that was separated from the guestroom by a hallway. On the count of three, we mercilessly shot at each other. God, did it ever hurt when you got hit. The shooting was not limited just to us brothers. At the pool we also shot the people who dove off the diving boards.

Shahram and I are going downtown. As the bus pulls up in front of the Blue Star, a very popular appliance store in Abadan, Shahram decides to shoot a bald guy on the street with his slingshot. Being an excellent shot, he hits the man square in his head. We're hoping the bus leaves before the man can figure out what hit him. We're dead wrong. He sees us laughing and knows right away we have something to do with the welt on top of his head, so he jumps on the bus. As he gets on from the front door, we are getting off the back exit and running away from the scene of the crime like million dollar NFL running backs.

22

I've inherited my dad's good looks and many of his characteristics. Just like him, I'm very easygoing until I'm cornered or dishonored.

The year was 1963. I was 13 when a new family moved into a house across the street from us. All the neighborhood kids knew the man of the house was nothing but trouble because he was just plain mean.

For example, while playing soccer, if our ball accidentally went over the fence and landed in his yard, he didn't give it back to us. He'd cuss us out—something completely unheard of in our community—for having a good time or laughing out loud. And we couldn't do anything about it, because within that society, kids didn't question an elder. This went on until the man had to face my easygoing dad.

Mr. Golcheen, our new neighbor, had a dog that was just as mean as her master. One day the dog got out of the gated front yard and bit one of my brothers. After he came home crying, my mom approached Mr. Golcheen and very politely said, "Sir, you shouldn't let your dog get out of your front yard." To which, he very sarcastically replied, "Madam, you shouldn't let your boy get out of your front yard."

The poor soul wasn't aware that my dad, who'd just gotten home from work, was standing across the street listening to the whole conversation. Having his wife insulted demanded that his honor be restored, so my dad charged the man. That was the only time I remember my dad that angry. Fortunately for the man, other neighbors stopped my dad and allowed Mr. Golcheen to cowardly duck into his house. A few weeks later he moved out of the neighborhood.

The year is 2002. This is my daughter's senior year at Birmingham High, and her best friend has talked her into working with her at this dive of a pizzeria in a shady part of the city we live in. I'm not very happy with my daughter working in such a place, but Megan's excitement overrides her dad's disagreement. After all, like my dad, I'm also an easygoing father, who, as much as possible, never says, "No."

After working there for a few months, one night Megan comes home crying. The owner of the place, who has a very foul mouth, had cussed her out in front of customers. She doesn't want to work there any more. Many Americans would be quite delighted to hear their daughter isn't going to be working for a place they disapprove of and leave it at that. But not me! I was raised in a shame-based culture and taught to defend my family's honor, which is very important to me.

I call my good friend Dennis. He's of Swedish decent and is built like an 18 wheeler, burly and strong. I tell him what I'm about to do and ask him to go with me. He readily accepts my request. No sooner do I call and tell him my game plan, than he's at my front door. We get in his truck and head for the pizzeria.

I've met the restaurant owner before. He's a scrawny looking guy who was born in Lebanon but raised in America. As soon as I enter the place, he recognizes me and has a feeling of why I'm here. I ask him to meet us outside. We go out and I sit at a table with my back against the wall across from him. Dennis stands right behind him, just as we've planned.

"Are you going to beat me up?" he asks nervously, hoping I get his joke.

"Of course not!" I reply. I've no intention of beating anyone up. I just want to teach this spoiled brat a lesson and restore my daughter's honor.

"You know what 'aaibe' is, correct?" I use the word for shame in Arabic.

"Yes!"

"You know how important our honor is in that part of the world. You've brought 'aaibe' on my family by dishonoring my daughter, and that needs to be rectified."

"You're correct, sir. I'm sorry for using bad language around your daughter."

"You should never use bad language around my daughter period; but even more important, you will never direct it at her."

"I'm very sorry. Please tell her that if she comes back, I'll never do it again."

"That's never going to happen. She's not coming back to this place, EVER," I smirk.

My family honor is restored, and I'm satisfied. But, even more important, Megan knows that her dad stood up for her and that she can always depend on me to be her covering and protection.

As we're walking away, I thank Dennis for going with me, and he says,

"Thank you for bringing me along. I learned how my daughter should be treated."

A few weeks later, I hear that our Lebanese friend is fined heavily for allowing an underage employee to sell liquor to an undercover police officer.

23

Have you ever subconsciously set a boundary in your life? I'm talking about listening to that little voice in your head that says, "Hey, you can go up to that point, but don't you dare cross it." Or, "That's as far as you can go in your life." Ever wonder where the voice comes from? Who puts it there?

No sooner had my dad, with my mom's help, baptized me in the large pool, than I learned to swim on the shallow side of the pool. I swam as well as anyone my age, but with a limitation. For whatever reason, I'd decided that there should be a limit as to how far toward the deeper end of the pool I could swim. No one had told me that. I set the boundary myself.

Watching my friends, I used to envy them jumping off the diving board and having so much fun on the deep side. I knew I could swim as well as they did, but there was that marker on the edge of the pool that forbade me from crossing to the other side to jump off the diving board.

This went on for weeks. There was only so much you could do on the shallow side of the pool. You could swim the width of the pool, race your friends, and even wrestle them; but there was something about being able to go to the deeper side, something that initiated you into a new season of your life. Something that said, "Hey, I am all grown up now. I am not afraid of being in the part of the pool that, to touch the bottom, I need to be completely buried in the deep waters." And then one day I decided I wanted to cross the barrier. I so wanted to dive off the board like everyone else that nothing could stop me any more. So I did it.

I walked to the deep side of the pool, waited for my turn, got on the diving board, and dove into that cool water. I still remember the rush I experienced as I sank deep with the waters over my head. Suddenly I had a great epiphany: if you can swim, it doesn't matter how deep the waters are, you will always float to the top.

Within a few seconds I was back on the board again for more and more dives. Needless to say, I didn't stay in the shallow end of the pool anymore. Who knows; if I'd not overcome the fear of crossing that artificial boundary that I'd created for myself, I may have never accomplished one of the greatest achievements of my life. But I have to admit, there are still self-made limitations in my life that I struggle with regularly.

24

I'd never seen a picture of a naked woman till I was **in the eighth grade.** It was the first period in the afternoon. As we're waiting for the teacher to show up, the guy next to me put a book in front of me and opened it to the page with the picture of a nude woman. I was so shocked by the photo that I let out the loudest yell any man my age could muster up. Unfortunately my screaming took place a split second after the assistant principal had entered the classroom—when the whole class had gone dead silent. But the black and white photo of a nude woman had so overwhelmed me that I didn't notice his presence. He wanted to let us know that our teacher was going to be late.

The assistant principal, or *naa-zim,* was a mean, heavyset, tall man with pockmarks on his face. He always carried a whip made out of several strands of heavy electrical cables. We called him Gurgo, the Persian name for Godzilla.

"Which one of you screamed?" he asked sternly.

Everyone looked my way. I'd no choice, so I raised my hand.

"Why did you scream, boy?" he asked with fire gushing out of his eyes. I still remember that scary look. I had no answer. I wasn't about to squeal on my friend who'd just introduced me to the picture of a naked woman, so I didn't say anything.

"Come with me," barked Gurgo.

He took me to his office where I was commanded to hold out my hands, and I received three most painful lashes on each hand with his whip. I don't know if the pleasure of seeing a naked woman for the first time in my life was worth the pain of those lashes.

25

"**W**e're going to have a race, and the winner will get a Coke and a cupcake," announced the teenager in charge of our summer activities. Every summer the oil company put together different types of activities for the school-age kids—activities like swimming, tennis, horseback riding, outings, and movies. On this day the kid in charge of the group decided to have a bunch of us swim a lap against each other. We did, and a few minutes later I was enjoying my Coke and cupcake. This was the beginning of many more competitions to come.

In those days during the summer, all the swimming pools in the city had competition days where swimmers competed in various races, diving, and water polo. I looked forward to those days. It wasn't unusual for my friends and me to show up at these events just to be spectators, not planning to participate in races. And, since I had no intention of competing, I wouldn't even bother to take my trunks with me. But no sooner would we get to the pool, than I found myself looking around to see if I could borrow

someone's swimming suit to participate in one or two of the events.

Up to this day my mother still reminds me of all those summer evenings when I came home from an event and quietly pulled a trophy or a medal out of my pocket to surprise the whole family.

26

Shahriar's idol was Dr. Kildare. For as long as I can remember, my second brother always wanted to be in the medical profession. Imitating the popular TV doctor of the early '60s, Dr. Kildare, Shahriar would wear his pajama top backwards, so, like Dr. Kildare's uniform, he could have a turned around collar. His love and passion for the medical field later led him to study pharmacology and become a successful pharmacist in the U.S.

My uncle Sia was my idol—my artistic uncle, a civil engineer who was married to my aunt Parichehr. He was the bad boy of our time. He had impeccable taste when it came to clothing. All his shirts were cut European style with darts in the back. He rode a motorbike, dressed like a movie star, and was an excellent dancer.

He must have been the inventor of the game Pictionary. All the boys would gather around him while he drew different famous characters as we each tried to guess what he was drawing before the drawing was completed. I longed to have his talent and to one day become an engineer like him. Not once did I realize that I wasn't created like him. I thought with higher education, one day I'd be just like him.

Within the Iranian school system, depending on your grades in junior high, you spent the high school years majoring in math, biology, or literature. If you wanted to study engineering in college, you had to have been a math major in high school. As hard as tried—my parents even hired tutors for me—I never mastered math in junior high and consequently wasn't eligible to major in math at high school. So, for me, there was no hope of becoming like Sia.

I can't describe the pain and the shame I experienced before all my peers who did become math majors. I was ashamed of letting my parents down and felt like such a failure. In fact, the emotional stress of this disappointment impacted my life to such a degree that I gave up swimming competitively. All my success in swimming couldn't wash away the shame that came with lack of educational success.

It still pains me when I think about those days. But as my dad once said about me, "What he lacks in intelligence, he make up in perseverance." However, my problem wasn't lack of intelligence but my short-term memory, especially when it came to math.

Like most Iranian students, I used to stay up all night studying under the streetlight or on the front porch where it was quiet, pacing back and forth memorizing formulas, events, or phrases. But in the morning I could barely remember what I had studied. By the way, I still have the same problem today. While driving, my wife, Karen, once said that if it weren't for her, I'd end up in Timbuktu.

In tenth grade I studied biology; but after studying my heart out, I finally was able to pass a test that made me eligible to study math for my last two years of high school. In that same year I started attending a private school. Those two last years were nearly hell since every class was math oriented, but I persevered and passed them by the skin of my teeth. That was just the beginning of the battle in becoming like my idol, Sia.

27

It was a couple of days before a swimming event at our neighborhood pool. At every event several hundred people from all over the city came to watch us compete. The workers were busy setting up bleachers around the pool. All my brothers, friends, and I were so excited. We were all talking about which event each of us was going to participate in and what we were doing to prepare ourselves for it.

"To have enough energy, I'm going to eat a lot of dates right before my event," one would say.

"Make sure you don't lift any weights. Weight-lifting and swimming just don't go together," another piped in.

There were no trainers or coaches to teach us what to do. Sometimes I wish we had trainers the way American kids have them today. I might have become a much better swimmer. On the other hand, we swam because we loved the sport. Winning or losing was not so much of an issue for us. It seems to me that today, the fierce competition in every sports activity and the amount of time that one spends preparing for it just sucks the joy out of playing the game, especially for little children.

I was participating in the 200-meter backstroke. All my other competitors were a few years older and much bigger than I. My biggest supporter was my mom. As the race began, I could see her walking along the edge of the pool encouraging me to go faster—something that was not allowed, but nobody dared to stop her. I came in third that day, and everyone was so happy for me. I still have the photo of this skinny dark-skinned boy standing on the third-place platform with my aunt and other people behind me screaming their heads off.

It's my son, Todd's, first year at junior high. He's six-feet tall, a head and shoulder over all his classmates, but weighing only 120 pounds. We decide it's time for him to join a Little League Christian baseball team in the neighborhood. He's never played the game with a team, but I figure he's only 13, and it's not too late to learn how to play the game. What a big mistake. This is not Iran. This is America. Winning's not everything. It's the only thing.

Ten minutes into the first practice day, it's obvious that the kid who's taller than everyone else couldn't hit, catch, or field a ball if his life depended on it. Prior to the second practice meet, the coach, a balding fat guy, pulls me aside. Pointing at the kids in the field, he says, "You see these kids; they've been playing the game since they were in first grade, and your son's no match for them."

I know what he's trying to say, albeit in a very cowardly way. Todd's going to hold the team back, and they might not make it to the playoffs.

"Sir, something really sucks to no end when you say a 13-year-old is considered to be too old to start something new in his life. Whatever happened to playing the game for fun? Is winning all you care about?" I say with disgust.

"I agree with you, but that's the reality."

"Well, we're not giving up."

It's the third day of practice. As Todd and I are sitting in the car waiting for the team to show up, I notice my son is shaking.

"Why are you shaking, son?"

"I don't want to go on the field. I'm not good at baseball."

"I thought that's what YOU wanted."

"No dad, I thought YOU wanted me to play baseball. I'm doing it for YOU."

"To hell with this! I want you to have fun like I did when I was your age. I didn't swim for my parents. I swam because I loved the sport. You don't have to do this for me."

I get out of the car, walk up to the coach, and tell him we're not coming back. He says he knew we'd quit sooner or later and hands me my check back. He never deposited Todd's registration check. I still have the check.

Just seven years later, Todd's a candidate in the mayoral race for the city of Azusa, a major city in Southern California. His opponent, the incumbent mayor, is a 50-year-old Hispanic lawyer lady. Todd is only 20 years old. If he wins, he'll be the youngest mayor in the history of California. He has his own election committee and is campaigning like a seasoned politician. Papers are writing about him, and he is on the news. He loses by several hundred votes and comes in second.

28

he summer I turned sixteen, an older friend, Nersi, encouraged me to enter a 100-meter butterfly event that was taking place at our neighborhood pool. I could swim all the strokes pretty well, but the butterfly, the hardest stroke, was not my favorite. Nevertheless, I took his advice and swam the race winning first place. It was then that I realized I was a natural.

In 1976 I became the city, and later the state, champion and eventually went to Tehran, the capital of Iran, to compete in the national high school swimming championship. That year I won a silver and bronze medal.

A few weeks later I became eligible to represent our state in the national championship. I had fairly won my place on the team, but for political reasons the team's coach decided not to take me along. He was playing favoritism and wanted to take one of his friends in my place.

After my dad and mom talked it over, my dad called up the coach. He first suggested that the coach include me with the team and my parents would pay my way. When the man refused, my dad told him, "My son is going to swim on the team whether you like it or not, even if he has to swim in an undesignated lane."

The coach, a blue-collar employee of the oil company, knew he could not argue with my dad. For one thing he was clearly wrong, but he also knew who my dad was and what position he held at the company. Up to this day I don't have any idea why he'd made such an asinine decision, since they had no one else on the team to swim the event as well as I did. That year I became a national champion winning third place in 100-meter butterfly. I also received a silver medal for swimming in the relay event.

The Amjadiyeh pool in Tehran is an Olympic-size pool with a 10-meter diving board. I've never experienced jumping off a 10-meter board—our diving boards in Abadan only go as high as 3-meter. Between the heats I decide to add one more experience to my life and climb up that monster of a diving board.

I have a fear of heights, especially when I'm on top looking down. It takes me what seems like a lifetime to get to the top. I stand on the top for a while contemplating my stupid decision. Climbing down is no option. People are watching me down below. So, I do what every self-respecting man in my position should do—jump.

Coming down I'm tilted a bit to the left, so my entry is anything but clean. I hit the water so hard it knocks the wind out of me. As I'm climbing to the surface to catch my breath, surprisingly I notice I can move my legs very freely. The impact is so hard it's also ripped my trunks off. I come to the surface butt naked. I have to beg a friend to bring a towel to the edge of the pool so I can wrap myself in it before getting out.

29

There were only 15 students in my graduating class. We didn't have proms in Iran; so after graduation, to celebrate—except for two of us—the whole class went to Abadan's infamous house of prostitution. Even as a young Muslim man, I had high moral standards that set me apart from majority of my peers.

It was common for men in Iran to make cute comments, *maataalack*, while passing women on the streets. Some young men also followed random women off the street to learn where they lived in the hope of befriending them later. I never participated in such activities.

Early on in life, mostly out of pride, I decided that I wanted for women to notice me and not the other way around. My friends often ridiculed me, since, according to them, I was too ignorant to know how to undress a woman with my eyes. What they did not realize was that it was my pride and respect for women that prevented me from doing so. In fact, I have a broken nose to prove it.

When sharing a ride on a friend's bike, we did not sit on the handlebars. Rather, we side-saddled on the support-bar that goes across a boys' bicycle. One day, after hours of playing basketball, my friend Albert was taking me home on his bike. As we're turning the corner on my street, he noticed a group of girls riding their bikes ahead of us.

"Let's follow them," Albert suggested.

"No," I replied.

But he continued to follow them anyway. That was when I stuck my foot in the spokes of the front wheel, attempting to stop him. Immediately the back wheel lifted up, and I was thrown, face down, to the pavement. As my face was bouncing back up, Albert landed on me and smashed my face into the pavement for the second time. Consequently, in a few minutes I looked as if Mohammad Ali had mopped the canvas with my face, and I ended up in the emergency room with a broken nose and a concussion.

30

fter graduation I had three choices: get into a university, get drafted, or go abroad to school. Due to a shortage of universities, only the very elite or the most connected students could pass the entrance exams. I was neither.

Since I had started a year early, I had a year to figure out what I wanted to do before getting drafted. By this time some of my classmates had already left for England. My uncle Sia had come to the U.S., and I wanted to follow in his footsteps.

During the Shah's regime, Iran was America's greatest ally in the Middle East, which made it quite easy for Iranian students to obtain visas to the U.S. Every year the whole country made a big deal of the students coming home from America for their summer vacations. I still remember the photo in a local paper of several students getting off the plane in Tehran Airport, waving their cowboy hats at the people greeting them. I wanted to be one of those students waving my cowboy hat.

My parents were quite reluctant to let me go to a foreign land all by myself. Today, being a father, I understand the reluctance. But at the time, like most teenagers, I looked forward to the adventure of being on my own and away from my family. So I kept pressuring my parents.

In retrospect, I wish I had more understanding of my parents and brothers. I wish I had been less demanding towards my whole family. But at that time I longed to be honored; and for me, attaining higher education was the way to go. I had to prove to everyone around me that I deserved his or her respect by getting my degree in engineering, a degree that was totally math-oriented. I wanted to be the one who, when rebuking his underachieving son, my next-door neighbor would say, "*Khaak baar saaraat! Cherah toe mess-leh Shahrokh neestee?*" Literally translated that says, "Dirt on top of your head (shame on you). Why can't you be like Shahrokh?"

My parents' reluctance also had to do with finances. We were not a rich family. When I finally convinced them to send me overseas, my dad had to travel to Tehran to secure a loan for me. In fact, as my plane left Abadan Airport for Germany, my dad was still in Tehran finalizing the loan. I didn't get a chance to say goodbye to him.

As it was the custom, many of my parents' friends came to see me off. What a drastic contrast between then and now, when you just drop the person you're seeing off in front of the terminal and leave as quickly as you can lest you're given a ticket for staying at the curbside too long.

Our friends were literally standing on the tarmac as my plane took off. It was just like a scene out of the movie *Casablanca*, as Humphrey Bogart said goodbye to Ingrid Bergman.

With a lot of hope and the promise that I would soon be back to make my family proud of me, I waved goodbye. Little did I know that would be the last time I would see Iran.

In almost 19 years living in Iran, we only moved twice. The oil company provided the housing for its employees according to their pay grade. The rent was directly taken out of the employees' salaries; so as my dad was given a raise, we moved into a larger house.

The first time, we literally moved from our house to the one next door. Without informing the authorities, my parents switched houses with a group of single men who lived next to us. At the time I couldn't have been more than five years old, but I still remember the move.

A few years later we moved from one block to the next. Consequently, I had never experienced the awkwardness of having to get used to a new place, new neighbors, new schools, or new friends again and again, as today many kids in the U.S. have to endure.

But now everything was about to change. For the first time in my life, I was leaving my security blanket, my life-giving umbilical cord, my family behind me.

31

It was around 2 a.m. on May 24, 1969, exactly one month before I turned 19, when my plane landed in Los Angeles. There was no one waiting for me, I didn't know where to go, and on top of all that, I could barely understand any English.

All I had was the address to my language school, which I gave to the taxi driver. He dropped me off in front of the school building around 3 a.m. on 6th Street and Bonnie Brae in downtown LA. To no one's surprise, the school was closed. So the driver suggested I check into the hotel across the street.

When I look back, I see the wisdom in the idiom "ignorance is bliss." After living in Los Angeles for 40 years, unless I'm lost, you'll never catch me in that part of town after dark. The lobby was filled with people who were just hanging out. Later I found out that they were hookers, pimps, johns, and drug dealers.

The next morning I put on my suit and tie and went across the street to the language school, ESL. After I registered, I went to my class. The school had started a few days earlier, so I was the only student who hadn't been introduced to the class yet.

As I entered the class, my teacher, Lana Fisher, pointed to me and asked, "What's your name?" I jumped up to answer her, and the whole class laughed at me. You see, in Iran, when a teacher asked you a question, out of respect, you had to stand up to answer him. I didn't know that in the U.S. it was acceptable for the student to be standing on his head while talking to the teacher. However, up to this day, I have no idea why a class full of foreign students would laugh at me for doing something that they did in their own countries.

After I was over my initial shock of being laughed at, I had a conversation with Lana that went something like this:

"My name is Shahrokh."

"How do you spell that?"

"S-H-A-H-R-O-K-H!"

"What does it mean?"

"King face or face of the king."

"How do you pronounce that?"

"Shahrokh!"

"What?"

By this time I was so embarrassed for my teacher not being able to pronounce my name and angry with my parents for naming me Shahrokh, I said, "Just call me Shah," something that I'd never been called before. In Farsi "Shah" is not a proper name; it's a title that means "king." It's reserved only for the king of Iran. So, on my first day in

America, my name—my whole identity—changed. I became a king.

Since that first day in the U.S., I have been called a barrage of names such as "Shad-rack Ashfar," "Shamrock Assfart," or simply "Mr. Shhhhh," since most non-Iranians can't pronounce my first name. Many years later a friend who's a linguist tells me that in English there is no "f" sound before the "sh" sound, and that's why, even when looking at my last name, the Americans tend to call me Ashfar rather than Afshar.

32

For the majority of Farsi speaking people, one of the most difficult sounds to pronounce is the "th" sound. The sound doesn't exist in our language. So, for most of us, "three" becomes "tree," "that" is "dat," and "third" becomes "tird." The funny thing is that we don't even hear the difference.

I'd promised myself I was going to speak English well enough so that no one was going to make fun of my accent. So, up to this day, when I hear a new word in English, I keep repeating it to myself till I can pronounce it properly; and I still consciously have to press my tongue against the back of my teeth to pronounce the "th" sound correctly.

I owe most of my English-speaking ability to a couple of things: first, being raised around English-speaking people and watching a lot of American movies while growing up in Iran; second, I'm indebted to all my friends and teachers at ESL, especially my first teacher, Lana Fisher.

One of the exercises in our language class was memorizing and practicing dialoging with other students. I still remember parts of a dialog taking place between a husband and his wife in a grocery store.

"What's for dinner tonight?"

"Chicken!"

"How about some asparagus?"

"Chicken and asparagus go well together."

Most students who started the language school with me were off to college within a couple of months, but not me. I stayed there for six months. I didn't think with my level of English I was ready to go to college. In reality, I was too afraid to leave the comfort of my newfound friends.

Originally I was accepted to attend a college in Texas. However, when one of the teachers warned me of how, those days, Texans felt about Iranians, I decided to stay in California and never left.

It's sometime in the late '80s after the Sunday church service when the members get together for tea and cookies in the basement. We call that "The Fellowship Time." Our Jewish Iranian worship leader, Dariush, and I are talking when a new visitor approaches us. He's a "one and a half generation" Iranian —he was born in Iran but raised in America; and like most of his generation, he speaks limited Farsi.

"Excuse me! In Farsi, how do you say, 'I can do all things through Christ who strengthens me'?"[1]

He wants us to teach him how to say Apostle Paul's famous proclamation in the New Testament.

Without planning it in advance, looking at each other, or missing a beat, on cue and with a thick Iranian accent, we both yell out:

"Eye cann doo al tings toroo keraist who esterengtens mee."

You should see the look on the young man's face, as Dariush and I are rolling on the floor laughing our heads off while trying very hard to high-five each other. We're shaking so hard our hands keep missing each other.

The kid's eyes are as wide as they can get, and his mouth looks like a "Q" missing its tail. He has no idea why we're laughing so hard. It's taken me many years, but I've mastered the English language.

33

My first roommate was Korean, a classmate we called Mr. Kim. Neither one of us communicated well in English, but we managed to get along. Our apartment was just a few blocks east of the school, a two-story building that was probably built at the end of WWII. It smelled like something awful and was filled with mostly Hispanic drug addicts, prostitutes, and families. Our next-door neighbor beat up his wife on a regular basis. Sometimes I had to pound on the wall to stop him from smacking the poor woman around. This wasn't what I'd pictured America to be like.

Every Wednesday night on my way home, I noticed a building on Sixth Street filled with loud music. I was fascinated by the place. I used to stand across the street and just watch the people sing, shout, dance, play their tambourines, and clap their hands. One day an Iranian student told me that it was a church. He then went on to say, "Can you believe this? What a difference between the way we do mosque and the way Christians do church?" He was not critical, just astonished. Mosques are usually very quiet and joyless.

One evening ESL's student advisor, Larry, asked me to meet him after hours in his office. As it was my Iranian custom, I wasn't going to meet him empty handed. So I took him some *gaaz*, a traditional white Persian nougat made with flour, sugar, and pistachios. I also took my medals, family photos, and a few other memorabilia and stuck them in a black duffle bag my dad had given me. The bag looked like something a thief carries the tools of his trade in. On each side of it, in Farsi and English writings it said, "Iranian Oil Company."

By the time I got to the school, everyone was gone, and the front doors were locked. I decided to go to the back of the building to see if I could get in.

A big mistake!

The back gates were locked too. As I made my way back to the front of the building, I heard a thud and a squeal of a car breaking hard right behind me. As I turned around, just a foot or two away from me was a police car that had jumped the curb with two cops jumping out of it.

"Get over here," one of them barked.

This was my first time facing a policeman in America. I knew I hadn't done anything wrong; nevertheless, I was about to wet my pants.

"What were you doing in the back of the building?"

With my best English, I replied, "I come here to see my friend."

"Who's your friend?"

"He is my teacher."

"Wha'cha got there?" he said, pointing at the black duffle bag.

"Someting for my friend."

One of the policemen grabbed the bag, opened it, and pulled out a gaaz, which to him must have looked like some kind of illegal drug with pistachios in it. After smelling it and going through the rest of my stuff, he put everything back and handed the bag back to me. In the blink of an eye, as quickly as they had appeared, they disappeared. I ran all the way home, hoping I wouldn't pee my pants before making it to my bathroom.

This was my first encounter with the American police, but not the last one.

34

Unfortunately, my parents and I had miscalculated how expensive it would be to live and go to school in the States. I was soon out of money, and with that came a new level of anxiety. I was quite conscious of the burden I'd placed on my family by coming to America, and I was now too embarrassed to ask them for more money. So I had to find a job.

My first job ever was working for a small chain of hamburger stands called the Dog House. I was taught to flip hamburgers and make pastrami sandwiches. It took me a while to realize that the chain was owned by a group of gay men. Besides this being my first job, it was also my first introduction to the gay community.

Coming from my shame-based culture, working with my hands was not an acceptable vocation. In Iran only uneducated and lower-class people worked with their hands. I hid myself from the rest of the Iranian students who walked by the Dog House every day on their way home from ESL, lest they saw me cleaning trashcans. I knew my dad would die a thousand deaths to find out that his oldest son was mopping floors and waiting on strangers. But to me flipping burgers was much less painful than having to ask my parents to send me more money.

My brothers and I take my parents to a popular chain restaurant in San Jose, California, for lunch. This is their first trip to the United States.

After we're seated, our server walks up and asks if she can get us anything to drink. She is a pretty blond girl in her twenties.

Looking at my dad's face, I sense he's not comfortable.

"Maybe he doesn't like the drink we ordered for him," I think to myself.

But the drink is the last thing on his mind. I've been away from his culture for 16 years now and do not have the slightest idea what's eating at him.

No sooner does the young lady walk away to get our drinks, than my dad can't hold back any longer. With an array of emotions, which include disgust, pity, confusion, and anger, he let's us all know what's bugging him.

"What kind of a father allows a daughter this beautiful to work as a waitress serving strange men?"

In his culture, it is an absolute disgrace for a man to allow his beautiful daughter to be a waitress. I'm so glad he never saw his oldest washing out trashcans.

35

Though I was a lonely person, I was never alone. I've got a God-given talent for making friends. Within a few days after attending ESL, I befriended many of the teachers, students, and the staff. Within a few months, I accepted a staff member's offer and moved into a new apartment away from that dreadful neighborhood. To learn English, I knew I needed to stop speaking Farsi and be away from the Iranian students. But that wasn't the only reason.

I wanted to hide from my Iranian culture. I was tired of constantly being scrutinized by my peers and having to live up to a standard that I couldn't measure up to. Embedded in letters from home were statements like, "So and so's son just got back from America, and after only six months he was able to get his master's degree. What about you?"

I knew that the boy had lied. That wasn't uncommon those days, but I was here and the boy in the letter was in Iran with my parents. Who're they going to believe? Once again I was a failure who wasn't able to learn English in six months, let alone get his master's degree. The weight of the shame I was feeling was unbearable. My only comforting thought was death.

In the new apartment I had four roommates. Three of them were Americans and one was a French student whose lifestyle mirrored Charlie Harper's of the *Two and a Half*

Men TV sitcom. Here I was, a man who was raised to have utmost respect for women, living with a man who saw them as nothing but pure sex objects.

This was the beginning of the feminist movement when, thanks to birth control, American women had come to realize that they can be as sexually active as any man alive. And my French roommate took advantage of every minute of it. I assume it was his French accent that made him so attractive to those women.

Almost every week a new girl emerged out of his bedroom. He did not care what she looked like as long as he could get rid of her before the next girl found her way to his bed. I couldn't understand why the women would oblige him with such ease. He eventually married Julie, a dear Catholic friend of ours who worked for the language school. She refused to sleep with him till he married her. I was one of his ushers at their wedding—my first ever Catholic wedding. I had way too much fun kneeling and standing during the ceremony, not having a slightest clue what was going on.

My friends and I are about to jaywalk in Tehran. In Iran everybody jaywalks. There are three people a few yards in front of us doing the same thing, two men and a woman. To an outsider, driving in most third world countries might look quite chaotic, but for us there really is an order to the whole madness. Crossing each other on the street, both the driver and the jaywalker time it so that they end up missing each other by a few feet or even inches—no harm, no foul.

But this day, as the three in front of us jaywalk, the oncoming car almost runs them over.

One of the men lets out an earsplitting profanity having something to do with the driver's mother. By the time my friends and I cross the street, we have all decided that the woman is a prostitute. "No man dares to use such awful language in front of a respectful woman," we conclude. We're taught to have an utmost respect for women.

36

Throughout the years I've lived in the U.S., I've had a bunch of odds and ends jobs. I flipped burgers, pumped gas, went door-to-door selling discount coupons for various businesses, sold clothing, was a teller in a bank, and—my least favorite—placing ads and brochures on people's doorknobs and doorsteps.

To get that job, daily I had to get to downtown LA at five in the morning to beat all the winos competing for the same position. There was no job interview. First come, first serve, and you got paid in cash.

We were given a bag full of printed material and a route. The object was to make sure each household on our route was left with several pieces of material we'd collated earlier. Since the majority of the crewmembers were winos and couldn't finish their routes, I often ended up taking over and making more money.

To beat the competition, I had to leave my apartment while it was still dark outside. One morning as I was walking towards the bus stop, from the corner of my eyes I noticed a car driving along side of me matching my speed. Before I could react, I had a shotgun pointed at my face. Again it was the Rampart LAPD.

"You move, I'll blow your head off," shouted the cop.

"Put your hands on the hood of the car and spread 'em."

This time I was used to it. There was no urge to wet myself. I complied, and he patted me down.

I was placed in the back of the car with the policeman sitting next to me.

"Keep your hands on your knees," he ordered me.

"Where're you going?"

"To work, Sir!"

"Do you have any ID?"

After looking at the ID I produced, he barked, "Spell your name."

I guess he figured only the real Shahrokh Afshar could spell his own name correctly, and with ease I quickly obliged.

Apparently there had been a robbery in the area, and I matched the suspect. Fortunately, after questioning me for a few minutes, they let me go. But after that incident, I realized the job wasn't worth getting killed over, so I never went back.

37

Foreign student advisors of different colleges often visited ESL to recruit new students. When one of these advisors offered to accept me at Pepperdine College located in Los Angeles, I jumped on the offer. I didn't know anything about the school and had no idea how expensive it was. I was just not happy to leave my newly found friends. In January of 1970, seven months after coming to America, I registered to attend college.

I still remember how lost and scared I was on that first day of registration. I hardly had to do anything like that in Iran. My dad took care of all that stuff for us. Here I was, a proud insecure young man who didn't know anyone at the school, barely able to communicate in English, and without an inkling as to how the registration process worked. Why didn't I ask anyone for help? one might ask. For one thing, I didn't know what to ask, and secondly, I was too proud and afraid to ask for help. What if I didn't phrase my question correctly and nobody understood my English? The whole process was extremely overwhelming to me. On top of all that, I was the only Iranian at that school. There'd only been one other Iranian student, but by then he was long gone.

I wish registration was my only problem at Pepperdine. Being a Christian school, the college required that every student attend the chapel services twice a week and take the Old and New Testament Survey classes in order to graduate. Halfway through my first day of New Testament Survey class, I was quite frustrated with how much the rest of the students knew about the subject. It seemed I was the only student who hadn't read up on the subject during the summer break, or at least I thought.

It took me a long time to realize that almost all the students in the class were from Christian backgrounds and all were familiar with the NT. It was like putting a bunch of Christian kids in one of my high school Islamic studies classes and expecting them to compete with the rest of us who were raised Muslim. However, my biggest struggle was with my math and science classes.

The college also required freshman students to live on campus. I had very little money to begin with, and having to live on campus didn't help. My roommate was David, an Indian from Hong Kong. I never knew who he was till one of the Chinese students from Hong Kong literally shouted in astonishment when I told him who my roommate was. "His father's one of the richest men in Hong Kong!" exclaimed the student. Throughout the following years, David and his whole family became an important part of my life.

_____

It's the height of the Vietnam War. Every day there are antiwar riots and demonstrations in different parts of the country. Like most college students, I'm all against the war. I love the black culture and want to identify with the black students. Pepperdine is located in South Central LA. A teenager was shot by the campus security the year before I start going there, so the relationship between the black and the white students isn't "friendly."

One morning as I come out of the chapel, I notice a group of black students lined up in the center of the campus with their fists raised and their heads lowered. I have no idea what they're demonstrating against, but I join them anyway, raising my fist to the sky with my head bent way low. Later on when the black students put the school under a lockdown, I stand by them. It looks way cool, and it helps me fit in.

38

College was a nightmare. Halfway through the semester I was flunking every class except one, PE. I took beginning swimming. I didn't know who to turn to. How do you tell someone that you have no idea what a "true or false" exam is? When I found out what it was, I liked it a lot. That type of exam works much better for a person like me with a bad memory.

One day as I was going to a class, I mentioned in passing to a stranger on campus that I was flunking my NT class and didn't know what to do about it. The following is something that is still quite vivid in my mind, and I'll never forget.

He was a kind black gentleman who was a few years older than I. He was sharply dressed in suit and tie, which distinguished him from the rest of the students, and he carried himself with an air of authority. Our conversation went something like this:

"I don't understand anything that goes on in that class," I told him.

"Have you talked to your prof about dropping the class?" he asked.

"No! Can I do that?" I didn't know there was such a thing as "dropping a class."

"Let's go talk to your teacher."

And then he took me to the professor's office, where, explaining my situation, he asked the professor to drop me from the class. That act of kindness, as simple as one might think it was, is forever etched on my very soul. Unfortunately my newly found friend and the professor neglected to tell me what "dropping a class" meant, so I continued to attend the class and suffer through it. By the end of the semester, I had one incomplete, one D, and an A for my three classes—the A was in my PE class. But it got worse.

The following semester I had two Ds and one A—I took the advanced swimming class. By the third semester I was put on academic probation. This was not because I didn't try hard. God knows that I did. I'd stay up all night taking uppers and studying, just to end up failing one exam after another. My brain simply couldn't process math, and my English comprehension was not that good for other classes.

It's the finals week. I need to stay up every night for the whole week studying. To help me stay awake, I ask a friend if I can use some of her diet pills, which she'd gotten from Latin America. They're called diet pills, but in reality they're amphetamines. Every time the thought of flunking another exam grips me, I pop another pill. The pills help me deal with my feeling of shame and give me a false sense of security. As long as they're working, I'm confident that I'll do well and my parents will be proud of me. By morning time, there are only a few pills left in the bottle. My friend's quite angry with me for wasting several weeks' worth of diet pills in one night. I could've died. I flunk the exam anyway.

39

I **wasn't happy working for the Dog House and needed a better job.** My girlfriend at the time had started working for the May Company, so I applied to work there. I got a job working in the college section of the men's department. It was there that I met Paul.

Paul, son of a pastor, lived with his Pakistani roommate. He and I became good friends. I'd often spend my weekends with Paul, his girlfriend, and his roommate. One Sunday he took me to a church. This was the first time I'd been inside a church for the regular church service. I don't remember much about the visit, except that the church was very bright and quiet with rows of empty pews.

Besides Paul and me, there were five other men who worked in that department, and they were all gay. One night Paul invited me to his house for a party. When I showed up, I realized that I was the only one whose date was actually a female. After being there a while, I pulled Paul aside and quite mockingly said, "Are you crazy? You should have invited some straight guys besides me. Can't you tell the difference between straight and gay guys? How come you invited all of *those* guys?"

Paul didn't say much to me that night, but the next day at work, he pulled me aside and very gently said, "Shah, I *am* one of *those* guys." I was both embarrassed and shocked. Embarrassed for being so cavalier in approaching the subject and shocked to realize the double life my friend was living. Since then I have come to know, like so many other men, he was struggling with his identity as a gay man and was doing everything he could to live a straight life.

The men I worked with were some of the kindest men I've ever met. Their motto in that department was, "You have to be crazy or queer to work here." And they referred to me as "the crazy one." They helped me when I needed transportation, loaned me money when I needed it, and helped me with my taxes. Eventually, when I got rid of my bike, one of them, Gary, sold me my first car for $60—a 1965 Corvair. I named it "Booger."

It's been a few months since I've become a follower of Christ. Paul is dropping me off. Just before getting out of the car, we have a spirited conversion, which ends up with me rebuking him harshly.

"How can you call yourself a Christian and be gay? What kind of a witness are you to your Muslim Pakistani gay roommate?" I say to him.

He looks quite rejected and wouldn't say anything. Soon after I lose contact with him.

It's been almost 30 years since that incident. I'm now employed by a mission organization as the Middle East coordinator. My phone rings. It's Paul. He's been looking for me for years. We're both delighted to have found each other. After the usual small talk, he goes on to tell me the following story:

"Do you remember the day you rebuked me for being a gay Christian?" he asks.

"Yes, I do."

He continues, "A few weeks after that incident, one Sunday at church when the preacher gave an altar call, I went forward and rededicated my life to Christ. However, I want you to know that I'm still gay."

How long after a gay man becomes a Christian should he stop being gay? Some are quick to answer "immediately," because the Bible says,

> Or do you not know that the unrighteous will not inherit the kingdom of God? Do not be deceived; neither fornicators, nor idolaters, nor adulterers, nor effeminate, nor homosexuals, nor thieves, nor the covetous, nor drunkards, nor revilers, nor swindlers, will inherit the kingdom of God.[1]

Then, how long after *you* became a believer did *you* stop coveting or envying other people? After almost 40 years of being a believer, I still envy and covet. Does that mean there is no place for me in the kingdom? After all these years, I've learned to be more compassionate towards those who Christ died for.

40

When mortification gnaws at your soul like a sewage rat gnawing at a carcass, getting a letter like the following from your dad doesn't help much:

Dear son, I can't tell you how proud of you we all are. If I have to sell the carpet under our feet, I will do it to see you finish school. Your mom and I, along with your brothers, are all awaiting your return. By the way, so and so's son just came back from America with his doctorate degree, which he was able to obtain only after six months of being there. When will you have your engineering degree?

My dad meant well. He had no idea what he said was creating so much pain for his oldest, but that didn't help me any. I so wanted my family to be proud of me, but to no avail. I plunged into a deep depression and began thinking about committing suicide. Thoughts of death were the only soothing thoughts I had.

I know for most of my American readers this is a very hard concept to swallow. In a culture where independence is literally worshiped, in a society where as soon as one turns 18 he's expected to stand on his own two feet, it is difficult to picture a culture where one can be so dependent upon his family for all emotional, physical, and financial support. Americans can rail against their families yet still get mutual support and understanding from their friends, but this was not so with my Iranian culture.

Let me explain. If I decided to major in PE and got straight A's, my parents would not just be disappointed, they would be humiliated and shamed. Anyone who knew me would call my parents wanting to know why I was majoring in PE.

"Why don't you study something easier?" one could have asked me. "'Cuz there was no honor in something easier," would be my reply. Honorable things come with a price. I'd always believed if it comes to you easy, it's not worth doing it.

For the most part, the Western culture is founded on what anthropologists call "guilt base." In such a society there exists a measuring stick called the law which everyone most obey, otherwise he will be found guilty; hence, the term "guilt base."

On the other hand, the majority of the non-Western world lives in societies known as "shame base." In those societies living on the right side of the law has very little importance. What's important is doing that which brings you and your family honor. One will do everything possible—which could include, lying, cheating, stealing, and even killing—to prevent bringing shame upon oneself and one's family.

It's an exam day. I'm in the seventh grade. Not everyone cheats, but our teacher knows some of us will. To prevent that, at every exam he brings in a couple of his teacher friends to monitor the room. Wearing dark sunglasses, back and forth they walk the aisles, hoping to catch the cheaters. Many years later, sharing the story with some of my Ameri-

can friends, they ask, "If everyone knew cheating was wrong, then why did most do it?" Because getting bad grades is even more shameful than cheating. It's not breaking the law that we're concerned about, but bringing on the shame. However, getting caught was just as shameful.

Right after the exam, as some of us compare answers, others are comparing their cheating methods. The one who cheated the best is king. One has the answers written on the palm of his hand. To outdo him, the other rolls down his socks to show where he's written the answers. However, we all bow to the most honorable one who'd written all the answers on the back of his neck so even the one behind him could benefit. Yes, of course, I am exaggerating; but then again, I wouldn't be an Iranian if I didn't. We all know cheating is wrong, but the greater sin is to get a bad grade.

41

Although the thought of dying was quite comforting to me, I was too chicken to commit suicide. So I turned to taking drugs and cutting myself, and I bought a motorcycle.

My drug of choice was uppers because it made me feel like I could conquer the world. When I was angry with myself for failing, I jabbed myself with a sharp object. Watching myself bleed made me feel less guilty. That was my punishment for bringing shame on the family. When a classmate from Honduras offered to sell his 305 Honda, I bought it from him. Dying in a motorcycle accident wouldn't seem as bad as committing suicide.

By this time I'd moved in with a family that lived in Westwood, an upper-class neighborhood in LA's suburbs. I had no idea how to ride a motorcycle. The first time I rode it, I traveled all the way from West LA to South Central LA taking the side streets—I was too afraid to get on the freeway. I rode that bike for about 30 to 40 miles, which took almost two hours, killing the engine at every light and stop sign. I didn't know how to handle the clutch and the gas at the same time. However, by the time I got to school, I knew how to ride a mo-

torbike. Eventually I got on the freeway and learned to enjoy the wind blowing through my long hair. With my handlebar mustache, I was the Easy Rider singing Stephen Wolf's song, "Born to Be Wild."

It's been two years since I bought the bike. Tomorrow I'm selling it. Riding it is a mixture of fear and pleasure. I've crashed it a couple of times and gotten a moving violation ticket; but all and all, I don't find the bike to be a conducive means of transportation, especially when I have to pick up a friend on a rainy day.

I'm on my bike on the corner of Fairfax and Wilshire, waiting for the light to change. Knowing this might be my last chance, I decide to do something I've never done on the bike before—pop a wheelie. As soon as the light turns green, going north across Wilshire Boulevard in the middle of what's known as the Miracle Mile, I pop a wheelie passing May Company on the east and IHOP on the west. Holy Mother of God! I'm so scared after I land on the other side of the intersection that I pull into May Company's parking lot thinking my heart is about to jump out of my mouth. I'm so glad I'm selling the bike tomorrow.

42

I lived in the basement of a large house, away from the rest of the house. There was a second story room in the back of the house where the two teenage sons of the family and their friends hung out.

One afternoon as I was going to the kitchen, I smelled smoke. When I went out to investigate, I noticed smoke coming out of the kids' room. I rushed upstairs and tried to kick the door down, but to no avail. I ran down and called the fire department. By the time the fire department got there, the house had sustained much damage, and I lost everything. Thankfully no one was hurt. However, I had to move out.

Now, here I was, hopeless, scared, ashamed, homeless, penniless, and had just been told I cannot go back to school the next semester. They were kicking me out of college. Words aren't enough to describe the depth of despair I was experiencing.

A day after the fire, as I was sitting on a curb on campus with my arms resting on my knees and my head resting on my hands, a student who I didn't know walked up to me and asked if I was OK. Not that I meant to, but I must have look pretty pathetic.

"No, I lost everything I had in a fire yesterday," I told her. Without saying anything, she turned around went to her dorm room and came back with a cape and a sweater for me—hey, this was the '70s. I could get away wearing a lady's sweater or a cape. This was the beginning of my friendship with Ellen, the young lady who was going to be very instrumental in changing my life for eternity.

I was soon introduced to the circle of her friends who were different than all the other American friends I had come to know. They seemed to be happier and more peaceful than the rest of the people around me, two qualities that I so longed to posses. But this was not the first time I had noticed these qualities in some people around the school.

I played football or, as we say in America, soccer with a group of the students. One of the players was Doug, a longhaired American kid who was raised in Latin America. He was one foul-mouthed and bitter dude. He wore a headband and charged whoever was between him and the ball like a bull while cursing up a storm. I marveled at his skill to use the "F" word in some of the most unique ways I'd ever heard. He was capable of using the word between the "i" and the "t" of the word "it." I dare to say he enhanced my English proficiency by this unusual gift.

The following Monday he showed up at school with short hair and no headbands; and even more remarkable, he was very quiet and extremely polite. The man had literally changed over the weekend.

Doug walked up to me and said, "I was born again last Sunday."

"Ooookayyy!" I had no idea what he was talking about.

He then pointed to a red button on his lapel depicting a raised index finger with the words "One Way" inscribed underneath it. Then he asked, "Do you know what this means?" Apparently that was a rhetorical question because he continued, "There is only one way to God, and Jesus is that Way."

I still had no idea what he was talking about, but I certainly was extremely impressed with the change the man had experienced within only two short days.

Like most students my age, I am gravitated to anti-establishment leaders and identified with revolutionists. I've heard about Che Guevara, the Argentine Marxist, so I buy a book about him. I hardly ever read the book, but having it under my arm while walking around the campus makes me look cool—so I think.

This particular day, as I'm waiting to get into the chapel with the book under my arm, Tom, a guy belonging to Ellen's circle, asks, "Wha'cha reading, Shah?"

With much pride I reply, "I'm reading about Che Guevara, a great revolutionist," making sure everyone around heard me.

"Well, I myself follow the greatest revolutionist whoever walked the face of the earth."

"All right, up tight, and out of sight! And who'd that be?" I said, expecting to hear some communist.

"Jesus Christ!" is his reply, which leaves me speechless.

I've always known Jesus to be a great and kind prophet and healer, but never in my wildest imagination thought of him as some revolutionist.

For some odd reason, I just couldn't get away from these people who the rest of the school called Jesus Freaks. I kept coming across friends and strangers who'd gone through some kind of life-changing transformation that had made them more joyful with much peace, and it was all attributed to this prophet Jesus.

Since my bike often broke down, I'd hitchhike back and forth from South Central LA to Hollywood where I'd moved. One day a young man picked me up in his beat-up van. No sooner had I gotten in the van, than he began to tell me how Jesus had changed his life. I politely listened to him. As I was getting out of the van, I said, "Boy, it seems everywhere I turn, somebody's telling me about this Jesus." He immediately got out of his van, walked up to me, and, looking me in the eyes, said something that I never forgot, "Maybe He is trying to get your attention?"

43

My reaction to these Jesus Freaks was indignation. After all, "I belong to a religion that was God's final revelation to man with its prophet, Mohammad, as the seal of all prophets," I'd say to them. However, I couldn't escape one nagging reality. "How can a second-class prophet, namely Jesus, offer these men and women the joy and the peace that Islam isn't able to offer me?" So I continued to hang out with Ellen and her friends.

I started to attend Bible studies with them, but not because I was interested in the Bible. I had no idea what went on in those meetings; but as long as I was around them, I experienced a sense of peace that I so desired to take home with me. As much as I wanted to argue religion with the Jesus Freaks, they wouldn't get into it with me. In those days the majority of Americans had no idea where Iran was let alone what Islam was about. So, no one argued religion with me.

This unusual relationship went on for several months. I was being expelled from Pepperdine, and any hope of becoming an engineer was shattered. It was obvious that I was nothing but a failure, one who would never amount to anything; the oldest son who was an embarrassment to himself, his family, and even his people and culture.

I did everything I could to avoid all the Iranian students at school, whose numbers had grown by now. I was just too ashamed to even answer their simple question, "So, when are you graduating?" My life had boiled down to an agonizing pain of realizing my absolute worthless as an Iranian. I resented the culture I was raised under. But this was all about to change.

It's my first semester at Pepperdine, and tonight is movie night. I'm not used to the campus life and don't know what a movie night is, but I go to the chapel where a movie is being shown anyway. The movie is The Greatest Story Ever Told. *I've not seen it before and did not expect it to have such an impact on me.*

After the movie is over, I don't want to go back to my room to go sleep. Something is deeply bothering me. It was the scene about Christ's death and resurrection that's on my mind. "How can Christians believe that God Almighty would allow his sinless prophet, Jesus, to die such a shameful death and do nothing about it? How dishonoring is that?" I'm asking myself. As dangerous as it is, I decide to take a walk around the neighborhood, struggling with what I'd just watched.

44

once heard Billy Graham say, "The loneliest people on the face of the earth are college students." I believe the loneliest people on the face of the earth are the foreign college students. By some studies, the majority of foreign students in the United States never get to see the inside of an American's house before going back to their countries. But that was not my experience, and I had Kathy McCart to thank for that.

Kathy was our receptionist at ESL and one of my first friends in America. She had this uncanny ability to make friends with just anyone. Homeless people living in the run-down hotels around the school would come in to say hi to her, and she always made time for them.

On my second day at school, I needed an envelope to mail something; so I walked up to her desk, which was located in the lobby, and asked if I could have a "pocket." In Farsi an envelope is called *paakat*. Assuming it was taken from the word "pocket," I asked for one. Understandably she was confused. It took me a while to explain to her why I needed a pocket, but once I did, she taught me the word "envelope."

For whatever reason, Kathy took a liking to me, and I began to hang out with her and her friends. She and a group of the teachers worked part time for the Music Center as ushers. They used to take me to the Center where I got to see the plays for free after handing out programs to the audience. I had no idea what the plays were about, but I marveled at how the stage was all put together. Kathy also invited me to her home every Thanksgiving and Christmas. Except for two Thanksgivings, thanks to her, I have spent every Thanksgiving and Christmas with the McCarts.

1971 was one of the two Thanksgivings I didn't spend with the McCarts. That year it was Ellen who invited me to her home for a meal. She lived in Lancaster, a city about 80 miles north of the school. I rode my bike for two hours to get to Ellen's house.

As we sat around the table to eat, Ellen's dad did something I'd never seen anyone do before. He prayed over the meal, giving thanks to God for it. After eating a good meal, as Muslims, every once in a while we might have said, "*El-la-hee shokrat*," or, "Thank you, Allah," but never prior to the meal. There was nothing spectacular about the prayer, but for some unexplainable reason, it struck me like a run away Japanese bullet train.

That evening after the meal, I said my goodbye, got on my motorcycle, and headed home, riding as fast as the bike could go. As I was riding, I began to have a conversation with God. No, not the God of the Bible, but the only God I knew, Khoda, a contextualized mixture of the dualistic god of Zoroastrianism and Allah, the god of Islam. My conversation with him went something like this:

"God, I am a Muslim. I believe in Mohammad, Ali, and the other eleven Imams, but today I want to kill myself. Jesus, if you really are who these people tell me you are, I'll accept you…if you give me good grades at school."

I was not about to change religions or gods. However, I somehow knew if anyone could get me out of the mess I was in, it would be Jesus. There was no thunder and lighting, I saw no angels, and had no goose bumps, but I knew something had taken place deep within me after that prayer.

Evangelical Christians have a prayer called the sinner's prayer, which everyone who wants to become a Christian needs to repeat. Some Christians also believe that one should not make a deal with God in order to follow him. I am so glad there was no one around to put words in my mouth or tell me what to believe that Thanksgiving day in 1971.

I prayed to the only God I knew in the only manner I knew. At the time I didn't believe Jesus was the Son of God, that he was divine, or that he'd died for my sins on the cross.

Interestingly enough, as little as I knew about this man named Jesus, I hoped that he cared about restoring my honor just as much as my Christian friends believed in his power to forgive their sins. That's why I prayed the way I did. And though I prayed to Khoda, it was Jesus who came to my rescue.

The following day at school I went to one of my Christian friends, Tom Harper, and asked, "Tom, how does someone become a Christian?" I expected him to tell me anything from having to go before a priest to sprinkle some holy water on me while prostrating before a statue to shaving my head. But to my surprise, he said,

"All you need to do is to invite Jesus into your heart."

"Hey, I did that yesterday. What else do I need to do?"

I didn't understand the amount of joy Tom expressed by hugging me and jumping up and down. "It must be an LSD flashback," I said to myself. To him and the rest of the school, who heard the news within a few hours, I was now one of the Jesus Freaks.

It's the summer of 2005. I'm speaking on the subject of "honor and shame" to a group of pastors. As I get to the above part of my life story, I stop and begin to cry. Pastors are both moved and puzzled by my behavior.

"Do you know why I'm crying?" I ask them. Of course, they don't know.

"I just figured out why I prayed the way I did on that Thanksgiving Day in 1971. That day I was concerned not about my sins, but my honor. I didn't fear going to hell, since I felt I was living in one. What I wanted was for someone to restore my honor by changing my grades."

45

For many, coming to Christ is a process. Years ago Paul Hibbert, who at the time was the dean of the School of World Mission at Fuller Seminary, wrote a brilliant article entitled "Conversation and Cognitive Understanding." In it he asks his Christian readers the following provocative, and at the same time extremely challenging, question:

> Can an illiterate Indian peasant, Papayya, who could not pass even the simplest tests of biblical knowledge or theology, become a Christian after hearing the Gospel only once? And, if so, what do we mean by conversion? Papayya knows and believes in many of the 33 million gods his village's proverbs say exist, but none matches the God of the Bible.

The above question can apply to me too. Albeit I did believe in only one God, who I also believed to be the same as the God of the Jews and the Christians…but was he? At the time of my encounter with Christ, I didn't believe he was the son of God or that he was divine, and consequently, I didn't believe in the Trinity. I was taught that it only appeared to the Jews that Jesus was crucified; at the last moment God made Judas look like Jesus, and it was Judas who the Jews crucified while Jesus was taken up to heaven. So, was I a Christian? Did my conversion count or did I need to have a more complete theology before Christ would accept me?

There is a story in the *New Testament* about a man blind from birth who was healed by Jesus. In those days the religious leaders, called the Pharisees, didn't like Jesus very much. To them Jesus was way too rebellious to be who he claimed to be, the promised Messiah. So, when this blind man was going around claiming to have been healed by Jesus, the Pharisees accosted and questioned him. This is how John, one of Jesus' disciples, tells the story:

They called the man the second time—the man who had been blind—and told him, "Give credit to God. We know this man (Jesus) is an imposter." He replied, "I know nothing about that one way or the other, But I know one thing for sure: I was blind...I now see."[1]

I was that blind man. I didn't know Christian theology from a hole in my head. I didn't know how God could have a son or become a man. I didn't understand how one plus one plus one could equal one. I had a hard time comprehending how an all-powerful God could allow his innocent prophet to experience such a shameful and excruciating death at the hands of his enemies. But I could not deny the fact that from the day I made a deal with Jesus, I experienced a peace that surpassed my non-mathematical brain.

A few months later, in January 1972, I was baptized by one of the professors, Dr. Mitchell, at the church adjacent to the school. However, Jesus didn't live up to his end of my bargain. At the end of the semester I was kicked out of school.

A few months later, as I was sitting in the cafeteria of the May Company reading the *New Testament*—something that I had started soon after making the deal with Jesus trying to get to know him better—I came across Christ's interaction with Thomas, another one of his disciples.

Jesus had just appeared to Thomas who was not present the first time he had shown himself to his disciples after his resurrection. Upon hearing what had taken place, Thomas told the other eleven, "Unless I see the nail holes in his hands, put my finger in the nail holes in his side and stick my hand in his side, I won't believe it."[2] So, eight days later when Jesus appeared to his disciples with Thomas present, he told him:

"Take your finger and examine my hands, Take your hand and stick it in my side. Don't be unbelieving. Believe." Thomas said, "My Master! My God!"[3]

In that moment I had an epiphany, and in the margin of my *New Testament* I wrote, "Jesus is God."

I find it very interesting how little the majority of American Christians know about church history. Most Christians don't realize that it took the church hundreds of years to develop the Christology (study of Christ) that we so readily take for granted today. It's utterly unfair to demand that unless a person, such as me, doesn't exactly believe as they do that his conversion isn't authentic. Therefore, I believe it is only fair to afford us, who come from a completely different background, a bit of leeway; allowing us the same process the church went through before expecting us to believe in something that the Christians have accepted for hundreds of years.

46

I never got the good grades I'd bargain for and was consequently thrown out of school. But I was given something much greater—an unexplainable peace. That didn't mean I wasn't worried about my future. I certainly was. However, deep inside I had this confidence that all would be well. Regarding this peace, Apostle Paul says,

Don't fret or worry. Instead of worrying, pray. Let petitions and praises shape your worries into prayers, letting God know your concerns. Before you know it, a sense of God's wholeness, everything coming together for good, will come and settle you down. It's wonderful what happens when Christ displaces worry at the center of your life.[1]

The day I called on Jesus, He displaced my worries with a sense of God's wholeness, which assured me everything would come together for good. An assurance that all my sins, shame, and fears will be dealt with, or as we say in Farsi, I shall be *a-ghe-bat be khair* (my end shall be happy, blessed, or well).

There I was––a foreign student who was kicked out school due to lousy grades. I couldn't renew my student visa and was in danger of deportation. I had nightmares about being greeted by my family at the airport in Iran wanting to know where my engineering degree was. But on top of that heap of shame, I was now a *mortad*, an apostate, a traitor who'd turned his back on his religion, culture, family, friends, people, nation, and his God—or;

simply put, everything that comprised my identity as an Iranian Shia.

When a Muslim turns to Christ, he doesn't simply change one religion for another. Rather, he gives up centuries of what molded him to be who he is. I was more ashamed for my family than myself. There was a retribution for my action, which included my family. Now my dad, mom, and even my brothers had to bear the shame of not doing a better job of raising me as a Muslim.

Lying down on bed, I'm reading one of the Gospels, fighting some of my regular dark thoughts, "What if the Immigration Office catches up with me and decides to ship me home? How can I face my parents?"

I push the thoughts aside and keep reading. I get to the part where Jesus walked on water.

Maybe because I'm a swimmer or maybe because I've studied too much physics to know you just can't walk on water, whatever it might be, that act of Jesus makes a great impression on me.

As my thoughts drift back to what I was struggling with earlier, a still voice deep within my soul asks, "Son, don't you think the man who walked on water can also take care of your problems?"

I'm comforted by the question. I close my eyes and go to sleep. I know he'll take care of me.

47

In the '70s many hippies, such as my friends, became followers of Christ. Those who study Christian movements called us the Jesus People. One of the characteristics of Jesus People was their lack of compliance with mainstream Christianity. The majority of us preferred small home Bible study groups to more traditional Sunday services. For the first two years of being a Christian, I didn't attend regular Sunday services; and when I did attend church, it was a midweek gathering at Calvary Chapel in Costa Mesa, a church that met under a huge tent pitched in a parking lot, where I usually ended up sitting on a concrete floor.

The tent was always packed with longhaired hippies wearing tie-dyed shirts and skirts and patched up pants and overalls. There was always much joy in the air. I loved listening to Chuck Smith, a father figure pastor who spoke gently yet assuredly to us new believers. Those were some of my first regular encounters with American Christians.

I'll never forget the first time I saw a young man using his Bible as a cushion while sitting on the concrete floor of the parking lot. *What are you worried about that your torn dirty pants might get even dirtier? How dare you use the Bible as a cushion to sit on?* I thought to myself. This wasn't the way I was raised.

As a sign of respect, a devout Muslim will never touch the Quran without first washing his hands and won't open it without first kissing it and raising it to his head, allowing his forehead to touch it several times. So to watch Christians using the Bible, God's word, in such a disrespectful way was quite astonishing to me, an ex-Muslim.

I was quite vocal about my newfound faith. I had no problem sharing the story of how Christ had changed my life with anyone who was willing to listen to me.

Because for years strangers had given me rides when I didn't have any means of transportation, once I bought Booger, I decided to pick up anyone who was on the street with his or her thumb up. That was my way of returning the favor.

My passengers were my captive audiences. I don't think I was too obnoxious. I never had anyone saying, "Hey man, just let me get out of the car right now," because I'd offended them. But I was forceful. I truly believed that if my experience with Jesus changed my life that drastically, the same experience could change anyone's life.

I know there are Christians who have a hard time with the word "experience," since they feel a follower of Christ should rely on the Bible and not experience. But when you look at it, the Bible is nothing but an accumulation of man's experiences with God. What we know about men and women in the Bible is not so much their theological attributes, but their personal experiences.

Abraham is called the father of our faith[1] because of the way he interacted with his God. It was out of his experiences that David, the apple of God's eye[2], wrote many of the Psalms. Paul would have never written almost two-thirds of the *New Testament* if he had not first experienced getting knocked off his donkey by God and going blind. So I was no exception. I had a life-changing experience with God, which I wanted the whole world to know.

A couple of my Christian friends invite me to this meeting they are attending. The gathering is in a house where the living room is set up like a church with several rows of chairs facing a pulpit. Behind the pulpit is a gentleman preaching to those present. I understand nothing of what the man is talking about—by now I'm used to it. But those around me seem to eat it all up.

As the man is preaching, this beautiful, young, blond lady with her toddler sitting behind me asks, "What's this speaking in tongues stuff you're talking about?" Instead of answering her question, the preacher makes a gesture to a woman in the back of the room. Before the poor blond girl knows what's happening, several women surround her and take her into another room for what I later find out was prayer. I'm so glad it's not me who asked the "dumb" question.

The whole incident freaks me out; however, what happens next was even weirder. After a few minutes all the ladies emerge out of the room with the blond women all flushed and giggling. By then the meeting is over and we're having refreshments. I approach the lady wanting to know what's taken place behind the closed door.

"So, what happened in the other room," I quietly ask her.

The response sounds like something that my daughter used to make for the first two years of her life, "Lalalallalal-lalalalal." And for as long as she's there, the woman can't say anything intelligible. I know darn well it's time for me to get the heck out of that place when one of the guys who's brought me there asks, "Wanna get filled with the Holy Spirit?"

I quickly respond, "Maybe next week."

"But we might not come back next week. How about it?" he insists.

One of the downfalls of being raised in a shame-based culture is that you're taught not to say "no" to a friend even when every part of you wants to scream, "HELL NO!" Saying "no" to a friend might bring him shame and cause him to lose face. So, reluctantly, I agree. On the other hand, these are also people who've proven themselves trustworthy to me. I know they want the best for me.

As soon as my friend tells the preacher about my decision, just like with the blond lady before me, he makes his infamous gesture, which by now has become pretty familiar to me. Before I know it I'm being escorted to the scary sideroom by a bunch of old ladies.

The sideroom is a small bedroom where the ladies put me in the middle of the circle they create around me, and they all begin to speak like Charlie Brown's parents. I expect one of the ladies to say, "You're probably wondering why I've called you to this meeting," because I certainly have no idea why I'm standing in a strange bedroom with a bunch of old ladies.

I want to say, "Ladies, I'm just a visitor. Please let me go home in peace." But I can't. I don't want to let my friends down.

It's then that one of them commands, "Open your mouth and begin to speak in tongues!"

"But, I don't know how to speak in tongues," I want to yell at the woman. But she keeps persisting while the rest were sort of chanting, "Wawa wawawa wawa."

After about 30 minutes of praying for me with no result, they decide to take a break when one of my friends sticks his head in to see what's going on. It's late, and he wants to get back to our dorms. One of the ladies gives him the bad news, "No, he's not filled yet. There's something wrong." That is when a lightbulb goes on in my friend's head, like a neon sign on the top of a cheap motel in Las Vegas, and gives him a brilliant idea.

"He used to be a Moslem." My friend has just let the prayer warriors know what the problem is. And that's all these ladies need. Once again, with me in the middle of it, the circle is formed and the chant begins. But this time the women begin to pray in English attacking Islam.

"We bind the spirit of Islam."

"We curse whatever has a hold on this man," and,

"We loose the power of the Holy Spirit," are the type of prayers being shouted into my ears.

Standing there, I'm laughing inside knowing that my past has nothing to do with what's not happening. I keep thinking, "God, I refuse to fake it. If this is from you, you have to tell me what to do," when an idea comes to me.

"These women don't speak Farsi. Why don't you just say a few words in Farsi to satisfy them, and they'll let you go home?"

Something amazing takes place as soon as I open my mouth to speak in Farsi. Now I sound like Charlie Brown's dad. I begin to speak in an unknown tongue while simultaneously a warm tingling feeling flew from the top of my head towards my toes. I feel as if I've stuck my finger in the wall socket. I begin to fall, and the ladies catch me.

I later find out that I've just experienced what Christ's followers experienced on the day of Pentecost a short while after He had been taken up to heaven. I'm now a Pentecostal Christian.[3]

48

The first Christmas I was in the U.S., Kathy McCart **took me to her parents' house.** At the McCarts', besides Kathy, I met Lyle and Gretchen (her parents), her younger sister, and some other members of her extended family. I was quite fascinated by her cousin's ability to speak English. She was only five, yet she spoke English so much better than I.

Lyle and Gretchen are both products of the Depression era from Iowa. After WWII, Lyle, who'd served in the Coast Guard, was discharged in Southern California. Rather than going back to Iowa, he asked his wife, Gretchen, to join him in Long Beach. And a few years and a daughter later, they moved into the house they've lived in for over 60 years.

The McCarts had their own tailoring business. Lyle's a handyman who can fix anything that isn't computerized. He's a tailor, a mechanic, a carpenter, and a plumber— everything that I'm not. Though Gretchen never made it to college, she can put to shame many college graduates when it comes to general knowledge, particularly U.S. history. I don't know too many people who are as well read as Lyle and Gretchen.

Just like my parents, the McCarts don't have a bigoted bone in their bodies. Once, having gotten quite angry with a customer who'd told them a racial joke, they told him they didn't need his business anymore.

I hung out with Kathy and her friends a lot. One night about ten of us went to a Westwood theater to see the classic horror movie *Night of the Living Dead*. The only thing that stopped me from soiling my pants during the movie was having the assurance that the ten people on my row weren't zombies. In general, we Iranians aren't too big on spending our money on someone or something that can scare the crap out of us.

I'm planning to go to a movie with this girl I met at work a few months ago. She's a bit of snob and doesn't like to ride on my bike, so the few times we've gone out it's been in her car. She's supposed to pick me up at eight.

Eight o'clock comes and goes, and she's nowhere around. I start calling her, but no reply. Finally, around nine she answers the phone.

"Hey, I thought we were supposed to go out tonight."

"No! I don't want to."

"Why not?"

"Because, I'm sick and tired of you and your Jesus," and she hangs up on me.

I don't want to stay at home this Friday night, so I call Kathy.

"Hi Kathy, this is Shah. Wha'cha guys up to tonight?"

"I'm just about to step out with the gang," Kathy replies.

"Shoot, I hate to be this way, but wha'cher sister doing?"

"I don't know! Why don't you ask her?"

I've known Kathy for a few years now, but I only know Karen as Kathy's sister and nothing more.

A few minutes later Karen's on the phone.

"Hello!"

"Hi Karen. How'd you like to go out with an Iranian?"

Not knowing what Iranian I'm referring to, she asks, "Who is that?"

"Me!"

"Sure! When?"

"Tonight!"

"Tonight is too late, but how about tomorrow night?"

"Sounds great."

I get her address and directions to her apartment. I'll be picking her up at her place for dinner and a movie. Later on, Karen tells me she thought I was trying to hook her up with an Iranian friend of mine.

49

Karen couldn't make it that night, so we set a date **for the following evening.** I was to pick her up at her apartment in Westchester. She'd moved there to be closer to UCLA, where she was attending school.

Besides having a bad memory, I'm also bad with following directions. That night after getting off from work and driving 20 miles or so, I got to Karen's place. I parked Booger in front of her building, but could not find her apartment. She lived on the second floor of a fourplex; and, not following her directions, I neglected to go up the stairs.

I spent a whole hour going up and down the street and not being able to find her apartment. By the time I found a public phone to call her, it was way too late to do anything. So we planned to meet another evening. I guess that should have been an indication to Karen as to what kind of a man she was about to go on a date with—a man with no sense of direction.

It's my first date with Karen. We go out to a local Chinese restaurant for lunch. We're having such a good time that we plan to go to the Hollywood Bowl. She has two tickets for a night of classical music. She and her friend had planned to use the tickets, but for some reason her friend couldn't make it. We have box seats. It's clear that we're the only couple that has shown up unprepared. Everyone around us has baskets of food and bottles of wine. I decide to get

Karen something from the concession stand. All she wants is a cup of coffee. How difficult can that be?

Iranians are tea drinkers. By tea, we mean black tea and only black tea. Any other type of a tea is an abomination. We don't consider teabags, no matter how black, acceptable either. The true Iranian tea consists of steamed, but not boiled, loose tea leaves, which is served with a lot of sugar or sugar cubes. You place the cubes between your teeth while sipping on the hot tea. The process of steaming the tea is called "dam." So to get a good cup of tea you have to dam it!

Not being a usual coffee drinker, when I do drink it, I put a lot of cream and sugar in it. I assume Karen drinks her coffee that way. Boy, am I wrong. Karen, like many Americans, drinks her coffee black. So, after taking a few polite sips of what must taste like a "dam" cup of coffee, she puts the cup aside. I decide to finish the cup for myself. There's something wrong with the cream. By the time we got back to her apartment I have a severe case of diarrhea.

As soon as we enter her one-bedroom apartment, I rush to the bathroom, which is just off the living room, and start working on something that sounds like WWIII. I'm so embarrassed. To drown the noise I'm producing, I keep flushing the toilet.

When I finally get out, Karen wants to know why I kept flushing the toilet. Out of shear embarrassment, I can't wait to get out of her place. I quickly say my goodnight, and run out of her apartment like a gazelle being chased by a lion.

50

Karen and I started to see each other regularly. We both had a great time being with one another. She was brilliant, extremely well-read, very cocky, and beautiful, with long, flowing brunette hair that reached her waist. But, very important to me, she had an unusual sense of direction. You could take her to a place blindfolded, and she was able to find her way back. Before I knew it, I was madly in love with her.

Have you ever been in love? When you are in love you see the whole world through the eyes of your lover. You wake up thinking of her. Breathe thinking of her. Drink wishing she was with you. Food does not taste the same without her. Everything you do, you do with her in your mind. All you want to do is to please her. You can't stop talking about her to anyone who is willing to listen. And that's what I was experiencing.

Every once in a while when I went to see her in her apartment, as she was getting ready, I'd get the strands of her hair I found on her couch and kept them in my calculus book so I could feel near to her. One day as I was talking to my math professor, he reached over and, not knowing the significance of the hair, pulled the strands out of my book and put them in the trash. I almost screamed at him.

I know there are some Christians who believe we should not act according to our feelings, since our feelings can often deceive us. I don't have any problem with that; however, to totally deny our feelings is also wrong. After all, if the Bible commands us to love God with all our heart, mind, and soul,[1] then our feelings must fit in there somewhere. All my love for Karen, however, couldn't overcome one area of our disagreement.

Karen's parents had been raised as church going Christians; but once they moved to Southern California, they stopped attending church. Consequently, Karen was raised in a secular home. She was attending UCLA studying sociology, so believing in God wasn't a part of her agenda.

"If it wasn't because of your Jesus, you'd be a nice guy." Or, "How can you, a guy from a Muslim background, teach me about Christianity?" she'd often ask me.

What can I say? I was like the man who had just discovered a cure for his dreadful and deadly disease and wanted everyone suffering from it to try the cure. Often I dragged Karen to a church meeting under a huge tent and would have her sit on the hard concrete parking lot listening to Chuck Smith, hoping when he asked people if they wanted to receive Christ that she would go forward. But that never happened.

If I had only taken a look back at my own experience with Christ, I'd have realized that my decision to follow him didn't follow the typical evangelical norm. I didn't respond to an invitation given at a church meeting. I asked for Christ's help while riding my motorbike. No one dictated a procedure to me.

Unfortunately, I was blindly following those who knew Christianity long before I did. That was the way my mentors did conversion; and not knowing any better, I accepted their way to be the only way. Forgetting where I'd come from wasn't the only turnoff for Karen. My zealot's behavior didn't help either.

For Christmas one year, I strung out "Happy Birthday Jesus" made out of cardboard letters in Booger's back window. Every time the car came to a stop, the letters would bounce up and down and shake like a bobble-head dog in the back of a low-rider car in East LA. That infuriated and embarrassed the heck out of Karen, especially when we went to her aunt's house for a Christmas dinner.

I wanted Karen to become a Christian, but she saw no need for Christ in her life. I believe that Jesus offers a peace and joy that passes human understanding. But that does not mean that those who don't follow him have no peace or are joyless. I felt as if it was my job to convince her she lacked peace and joy, but she didn't believe she was missing anything. So we ended up arguing, eventually breaking up over and over again, just to get back together a few days, weeks, or months.

It's my first time having Karen over to my apartment for dinner. I've warned her about the way my roommate, Tom, prays over the meal.

136

"Please don't laugh when Tom prays. He's a new believer just like me. When he prays over the meal, he starts with the farmer who sowed the seeds, then goes to the baker who baked the bread and the butcher who slaughtered the cow and so on," I gently warned her.

Unfortunately, my warning falls on deaf ears. A few minutes into Tom's prayer, Karen is falling off her chair laughing.

Being Pentecostal isn't making things any easier between Karen and me either. At our Bible studies some people have started using their gift of tongues. The first time I take Karen to one of these studies, I'm begging God not to let anyone speak in tongues with her present. My prayers aren't answered. Brother Tom has a message from the Lord, which he blurts out in tongues, hoping that someone interprets it for us. Karen thinks he's praying in German and is quite impressed.

One evening after attempting for several times to contact Karen on the phone at her house, I became extremely worried and asked my roommate to give me a ride to her apartment. On the way there, I was so afraid something bad might have happened to her that I began to cry. My roommate, David, rebuked me, saying, "My God, if you care for her this much, you should marry her!" It turned out that Karen was spending the night at her parents.

51

It was around this time that my second brother, Shahriar, came to study in the U.S. and live with me. The day he arrived at LAX, Karen and I went to pick him up at the airport. It'd been over five years since I'd seen Shahriar. As I embraced him, I began to wail. Watching me cry, one of the passengers told his friend, "My God, it must have been a long time since they saw each other."

I wailed for a couple of reasons. I'd missed my brother, but I was also ashamed of my lack of accomplishments. I wanted to be the older brother who was picking up his younger brother in his Mercedes Benz—at the time, a status symbol among the Iranians—to take him to his huge house where Shahriar would have his own private room.

Instead, I was picking him up in Karen's '69 VW Bug to take him to my three-bedroom apartment where I lived with David and his two brothers and sister. I was howling because once again I was reminded of what a failure I was as the older brother. My Iranian culture demanded that I be "my brother's keeper."

The next morning after Shahriar's arrival, before I went to work, I asked him if he was hungry. He said he wasn't. Without giving it another thought, I left for work. In the Iranian culture, there is a tradition called *taarof.* Out of respect and politeness, one should never receive what he's being offered the first time he is asked. If the host offers the guest something to eat, the guest always refuses till he is asked three times.

After five years of living in the States, I'd forgotten the tradition, especially with my own brother. We never had to do that among ourselves. Needless to say, Shahriar was hungry when I asked him the first time, but out of respect for his older brother and thinking that I was going to ask him a second time, he'd refused my first offer. He went hungry all day. After that first day Shahriar learned very quickly to accept the offer for food and drink on the first try, and when he was hungry, to raid the refrigerator.

——————————

It's a nice summer day just a few days after Shahriar's arrival in the U.S. We're sitting around the pool in our apartment. One of the habits we developed as Abadanis is to be trusting of people, particularly Westerners. So before Shahriar goes for swim and without a second thought, he takes off his expensive watch and leaves it on his chair. A few minutes later he informs me that his watch is gone.

I've been watching the neighbors who're around the pool, so I immediately go to the apartment of the couple who'd just left the pool. They live on the second floor. Their door's open. Without any announcement, I walk in. My brother's towel and watch is on a table next to this huge man sitting on a chair. I can tell he's stoned out of his mind.

I walk up to the guy, pointing to the watch, and say, "You took my brother's watch."

"No, that's my watch, man," with his eyes half shut, he whispered.

By now, I'm pretty angry. "Listen man, you even took my brother's towel when you took his watch," I almost scream at him.

I'm not about to let this guy ruin Shahriar's first week in the U.S. The man's girlfriend pipes in, "He didn't know the watch was wrapped in the towel. He took the towel by mistake." She's lying.

I pick up the watch and the towel and with my head held high, I walk out. Once again, I've protected my little brother.

I might have suffered a bit coming to this country by myself, but it was not all in vain. Today all my brothers, who came to the U.S. after me, will tell you that I was the one who opened the door and made it somewhat easier for them to adapt to their new world.

52

Have you seen the movie *My Big Fat Greek Wedding*? That's a great depiction of my family and Karen's. My side of the family is loud, rambunctious, and, at times, pretty crude. Karen's is extremely quiet, reserved, and proper.

Karen's dad, Lyle, didn't like me. Besides the fact that I was about to take away his little daughter from him, he also didn't like me because I was an absolute moron when it came to being a handyman. Being the product of the Great Depression, Lyle is independent and self-reliant. He's a man who knows how to fix anything and everything.

By the time I met Karen, Lyle and Gretchen worked six days a week, ten hours a day running their successful tailoring business. In the evenings and weekends, Lyle was a carpenter remodeling the house—all the wood paneling in their home and the wooden shutters on every window were made by Lyle; and the huge carpet covering their living room floor for years was woven by Gretchen. On most weekends Lyle was a mechanic working on neighbors' cars. On the other hand, I was raised in a society where only lower-class people worked with their hands. We were never encouraged to learn how to work on cars or learn carpentry.

As my dad's leaving for work one morning, he notices his rear tire on the driver side is flat. He asks one of the neigh-

bors for a ride and tells my brother and me to fix the flat. Eight hours later when my dad gets home, his two teenage sons are still trying to figure out how to change a flat tire.

Cars have always been a mystery to me. The few months I worked as a gas station attendant in the Wilshire district, I managed to screw up things as simple as adding transmission fluid to patrons' cars. I put regular oil in transmissions and transmission oil in engines. I'll never forget the look on the black gentleman's face when he found out I'd just put regular oil in the transmission of his brand-new white Cadillac.

The first time Lyle looked under the hood of Booger and saw all the loose hoses and wires, he gasped for air, and exclaimed, "My God! I'm amazed that this thing even runs!" I didn't blame him. Under that hood everything was drenched in oil. Even though Lyle never cussed, I could imagine him thinking, "*Damn! Is my daughter going to marry this idiot?*" In short, I was the antithesis of all that my future father-in-law was.

53

I love to dance. Growing up, we danced a lot. I still can do a pretty mean Twist, Funky Chicken, and Shing-a-ling. That was one of the reasons I was so attracted to Karen. She danced like she had some black blood in her.

During the first few months of our relationship, we used to go to parties where we danced a lot. So the day I told her we're going to a party on the coming weekend, she assumed we're going to a *party*. What I'd neglected to tell her, albeit quite innocently, was that we're going to a Christian couple's house for dinner.

That night when I went to pick her up, she had dressed up for a *party*; so when I said, "Please bring your Bible," all hell broke loose. Up to this day, she accuses me of setting her up. We fought up to the time I knocked on my friend's front door. But everything changed when Jim, our host, opened the door.

Karen had been around some of my Christians friends who were quite immature. She'd noticed how some of those kids stayed up all night praying. They would do well on their exams the next day, but they never studied. What really made her disgusted was how my friends bad-mouthed their parents for not being born-again Christians.

Besides feeling that I'd been less than genuine with her, she wasn't looking forward to spending a whole evening with those immature kids. However, Jim and Dolly, my married friends, were quite different. I met Jim in one of my classes at Pepperdine. He was a Vietnam vet who had survived being blown up in Nam. He was an established family man who, along with Dolly and their two sons, took their responsibilities in life seriously. Although that night they'd invited other Christians from school, except for Karen and I, no one else showed up.

According to Karen, as soon as Jim opened the door, a great sense of peace came upon her, which ended the resentment she'd been feeling. We had a great dinner, and the conversation was quite stimulating. Their two little boys helped even more to put Karen at ease. As we were having dessert and talking around the dining table, Dolly, very casually, asked Karen what by now we refer to as "the very famous question":

"Do you want to get baptized with the Holy Spirit?"

Karen hesitated and said, "OK, I guess I can do that." And Dolly began to pray for her.

Pentecostal Christians refer to the baptism of the Holy Spirit as "the second experience"— the born-again experience being the first one. They believe one becomes a follower of Christ first and then comes the infilling of the Spirit. There's a "step one" followed by "step two"—a norm which God will not deviate from. The reasons for that argument are as follows.

The 66 books of the Bible bind God's actions, according to many Christians. He will not operate outside that boundary. He should do everything exactly the way he did it in the Bible. For example, going through the Book of Acts, a historical record of life of the church after Christ's ascension to heaven, the Pentecostals contend that every incident of the believers' experiencing the infilling of the Spirit was subsequent to the public declaration of their faith in Christ. Hence, they're born-again first and then filled with the Holy Spirit. Therefore, in order to be baptized with the Spirit, one has to first repeat the sinner's prayer—make a public confession of his faith in Christ.

I prefer not to handicap my Creator. According to John, Jesus' apostle, all the books in the world can't contain what Christ performed in his lifetime.[1] Although there is a bit of hyperbole in that statement—hey, John was from the Middle East where exaggeration is a part of life—it still begs the questions: If all the books in the world couldn't contain what Jesus did in only some 33 years or so, how could we limit all that God's done since the Creation to only 66 books? Is it possible that He might have done many other things that were never recorded in the book? As far as I'm concerned, my God is bigger than the Bible, and to limit him makes my Lord too insignificant.

That night Dolly didn't ask Karen if she wanted to become born-again; she asked her if she wanted to be filled with the Holy Spirit. And after she prayed for Karen, something amazing began to take place. My rational and logical college student from UCLA had a physical experience that made her sound like Charlie Brown's mother in one of Charles Schultz' TV specials; she spoke in tongues. In doing so, she completely skipped step one and put a hole in my Pentecostal theology.

The very next day, Karen began to read her Bible, and within a week she'd read it from cover to cover. In all my years of being a Christian, I've never seen anyone read the Bible with such hunger and so quickly.

After all these years of being a believer, unlike so many Christians, Karen has seldom given up her God-given rational nature and isn't afraid to question teachings that don't make sense to her. This has been a great balance for someone like me who's prone to exaggeration and who at times is impulsive.

54

From that night on we stopped fighting about religion. After searching a while to find a church we could attend regularly, at their invitation, we ended up at Jim and Dolly's church. It was a black church in the city of Inglewood where Jimmy's uncle was the pastor. Karen and I and two other people were the only non-blacks. After attending the first service, we decided to join the church and became very active members for the following two years.

One afternoon Karen and I drove to May Company so I could pick up my paycheck. After parking the car in the front row facing Fairfax and the IHOP restaurant across the street, I asked her to stay in Booger and went to the fifth floor to get my check. I then went to the jewelry department on the first floor, where I signed over my two week's wages for an engagement ring with a very small sapphire and two even smaller diamond stones.

Karen was still sitting on the passenger side when I got back to the car. I opened the door on her side, knelt down in front of her, and putting the ring on her finger, asked, "Will you marry me?" Yes, that was one of the craziest things I have ever done, but it is also one of the fondest memories of my life. We got engaged in a parking lot.

Back at school some of my Christian friends were shocked that I'd rather impulsively asked Karen to marry me. They didn't approve of my decision. After all, a decision like that requires much praying, fasting, and consulting with wiser Christians. In fact, the leader of the group I hung out with approached me to convey his concern by saying, "Some of us are worried about your decision. Have you prayed about what you're doing?"

"Sure," I replied. But truthfully, I don't remember if I ever had.

Why do some Christians act as if they invented marriage? As if the only marriages that are blessed and lasting are Christian ones. Or unless you pray, fast, and spend a good amount of time seeking God's face, you definitely will end up marrying the wrong person. If that is the case, then how do non-Christian marriages survive? My Muslim parents have been happily married for over 60 years. They never prayed about who they should marry. In fact, as I mentioned earlier, the day my mother was born, she was set aside to marry my dad—no time for dating or fasting to seek God's will! This is called an arranged marriage. How biblical is that!

I'm all for seeking God's will, but I also believe that if I knew what God wanted me to do in every step of my life, then I wouldn't need faith. Life's a risk. Every time I breathe out, I do it by faith, believing that there'll be enough oxygen for my next breath.

On the other hand, I wish I had a penny for every failed marriage that was consummated because the couple thought God told them it was his will for them to be together. I'd own Microsoft today. By the way, the leader who was worried about me not seeking God's will for my marriage got married a few months after we did, and his marriage didn't even last a year.

55

It was clear I wasn't going to be Lyle's favorite son-in-law. Every time I went to see Karen at her parents' house, he sat on his chair with the newspaper covering his face, completely ignoring me. I would try to make conversation with him, but he'd only grunt a single word response. I usually spent those times very uncomfortable and quiet. So when Karen announced her intention of marrying me, Lyle's first question was, "What about school?" Once he was assured that we'd not get married till Karen was done with school, he told her, "I've bought some stocks in your name, which you can cash in to pay for a large wedding. Or you can keep them as your wedding gift, and I'll pay for a small wedding." This incident brought another revelation to light for me.

In the Middle Eastern culture, the groom or his family, not the bride, pays for the wedding. I wasn't aware that in the Western culture the custom was the other way around. Since I didn't have a penny to my name, I was quite grateful for that American custom.

A few months after Karen graduated from UCLA, we had our very small garden wedding at church. Karen looked astounding in her wedding dress made by her mom. I was wearing a tuxedo. My brother, Shahriar, my best man; Kathy, Karen's sister, the maid of honor; Karen's parents; Karen's best friend, Linda; her husband; Charles, my math professor; his wife; the school's student advisor's secretary; and her husband were the only people in attendance.

Karen had hired an old friend to be our photographer. In the middle of the ceremony, his camera broke down; and since our pastor had specifically told us that no one should take photos during the ceremony, we only have a few photos of our wedding. After the wedding we all went to Karen's parents' house for a BBQ, cake, and punch. And just like that we were married on April 20, 1974. By the way, that also happens to be Hitler's birthday—I didn't know this till the day before I got married. A Jewish lady, Margaret, a holocaust survivor who worked at the bank with me, told me about it.

Throughout our years together, I've looked back to our wedding day with mixed emotions. I wish I had asked my parents for their permission or at least informed them of my decision to marry Karen. Because of my failing at school, I'd withdrawn from my parents. It wasn't my parents' fault that I was lousy at school. They never forced me to become an engineer. But somehow, because I was ashamed of facing them, I'd cut off my relationship with them.

For years I also wished we could have had a larger wedding. However, today I'm so glad we didn't. What a waste of money that would have been. Not that the stocks Lyle gave us in lieu of the large wedding amounted to anything—it was worth only $600; but I marvel at young people who spend an equivalent of a hefty down payment for a house on a wedding that, in many cases, will only last for a couple of years.

I also wish I'd not been so obedient to our pastor, who, out of some self-righteous attitude, felt that taking photos in the middle of *our* wedding ceremony rained on his sanctimonious performance. I was even more irate when I saw the wedding photos of another couple that got married a week after we did. They had a huge wedding with lots of photos taken by several photographers before, during, and after the wedding. I guess they simply overlooked the pastor's mandate and got away with it.

A few months after we'd been married, Karen and I were visiting my in-laws. I am an occasional coffee drinker, but at that time I was even less of a coffee drinker than I am today. That day I was tired and needed a "pick-me-up," so I asked for a cup of coffee. Halfway through the cup the caffeine kicked in, and I began to talk a mile a minute, cracking one joke after another. I had Lyle rolling on the floor laughing his head off. That incident changed our relationship. Lyle became much more open and friendly. From that day on, every time we went to visit, which was almost every Saturday, Lyle would say, "We need to liven up this day. Give Shah a cup of coffee."

56

It wasn't long before Shahriar got to know some of my Christian friends. He attended Pepperdine for a while, and it was there that he found out I'd become a follower of Christ. Up to that point I'd kept it a secret from him.

As ridiculous as it might sound, I'd met Jesus in English. So my Christian language was English. The American Christians have their own language, which a friend of mine calls "Christianese."

Because I didn't learn Farsi Christianese in Iran and had five years of being immersed in English, I had no idea how to explain my newfound faith to my brother in Farsi. There are words and Christian concepts that aren't used in the everyday English language of non-Christians, let alone in Farsi. So explaining my faith to Shahriar, or for that matter to any Iranian, wasn't an easy thing to do.

"Is it true that you're now a Christian?" he asked me one day.

I'd now been openly confronted and had to face the fact.

"Who told you that?"

"Chester, at school; but I told him he was wrong," he replied.

"No! He wasn't wrong. I'm a Christian now." And then I proceeded to explain how I'd come to follow Christ. I don't know if what I shared made any sense to him, but it wasn't too long after that, that our parents found out about my conversion.

At this point of my life story, many Americans often want to know if my Muslim parents disowned me. They have the impression that all Muslim parents treat their children who have left the faith the same way—disown or, even worse, kill them.

Justifiably, my parents were unhappy and ashamed of my decision, but they were not about to deny their love for their oldest son. Their only explanation for my shameful act was, "He wants to be an American now." Or, "His girlfriend's parents must have made him change his religion so he could date their daughter." It wasn't too far-fetched for my parents to make those assumptions. According to Islamic laws, a Muslim man can marry a non-Muslim woman but not the other way around. So if a non-Muslim male wants to marry a Muslim woman, he has to convert to Islam.

Muslims, in general, believe that one is born into a religion. Your race, basically, determines your religion and not your beliefs and practices. If you're an Armenian or even an Assyrian born in Iran, automatically you're considered a Christian. Following the same logic a bit further, every American is a Christian. So, according to my family, Karen had been born a Christian and was the cause of my conversion.

This issue used to be a great point of conversation with Iranians who wanted to know if I *changed my religion* so I could marry Karen. When I simply replied, "No! Actually, she wasn't a believer until after we met," their reaction was like the robot in the popular '60s' TV show *Lost in Space*, "Cannot compute, Dr. Smith! Cannot compute!" To them, this didn't add up because Karen was born a Christian and didn't need to convert to it.

57

Maintaining any lasting relationship has its challenges. However, when you add cultural differences to it, it becomes an even more insurmountable and difficult challenge. After 36 years of being married, the fact that Karen and I come from such diverse backgrounds still plays a great part in some of our difficulties.

For as long as Karen remembers, both her parents worked outside their home; and after they got home, they both helped in making dinners and doing household chores. On the other hand, my mother has always been a housewife who has not worked a day outside the house. My parents' roles were always very clear—my dad took care of the business outside the house, and my mom ran the household. I never saw my dad wash a dish. Not because he wasn't capable or it was beneath him, not at all. Rather, it was because that would have been intruding upon what was my mom's job. So once we got married, I expected Karen (who, by the way, worked her way through *my* schooling) to be like my mom, and she expected me to be like her dad.

Another cultural difference, which haunts me even today, is the way we communicate. Iranians in general are less specific in the way they communicate. You often have to read between the lines to know what they're talking about.

"What time are you coming over?" one Iranian asks the other.

"Sometime after noon."

That could mean anytime between 12 noon to 12 midnight. On the other hand, Westerners are masters at being specific. When Karen asks, "What time is it?" She wants to know it down to the second.

"What time are you coming over?" Karen asks.

"I be there at exactly 12:35," my reply should be.

I'm prone to exaggeration. I have to consciously work at being exact. Exaggerating isn't done deliberately, but naturally. It is something that we're raised with.

"How many people have you invited for dinner?" Karen might ask.

"Ten to twenty! Somewhere around there," without much concern, I'd reply.

"So, should I cook dinner for 10 people or 20?"

"What difference does that make?"

And, potentially, that could be the start of WWIII.

I hadn't thought that far ahead of the plan; and when she asked me the question, rather than admitting that I hadn't thought that through, I got frustrated and angry. Even worse, there are times that I felt Karen was deliberately being so specific to point out my lack of ability to be specific, not realizing that just as I am prone to exaggeration, she is prone to being exact—she was raised that way.

As the years have passed us by, I've become more like Karen, and she has become more tolerant of me. I think that's one of the reasons our marriage has been, if you would, successful. I now have a great respect and admiration for Karen's sense of organization and foresight. Watching her all these years has taught me to strive to be more precise and organized, and Karen isn't as insistent on getting the exact time when asking me for it.

My daughter, Megan, has been taking Tae Kwon Do classes for several years now. It all started when Rick, her teacher, started to teach martial arts to the kids at his Sunday School. The class eventually got big enough that he moved to a studio. Throughout the years I've come to know Rick and his wife pretty well and consider them good friends.

Today Megan is receiving her brown belt. There's going to be a ceremony at the studio. Rick is quite excited about the event because his master is going to be there as the guest of honor.

The small studio is packed with parents and relatives of the kids attending the school. There's standing room only. I find a seat in the back of the studio and sit down with anticipation.

First Rick gives a little speech and introduces a guy who does a choreographed staff routine. Next, Rick introduces his master. He's a young man in his thirties, a very well-known martial arts champion who happens to be Iranian.

As he begins to talk, the young six to seven-old-year white belt kids begin to march in with their yellow belts in their hands. They are going to be promoted to yellow belts today.

As the kids march in, Hormoz, the master, asks the little boy in the front of the procession, "What color belt are you?"

I can tell the boy is quite intimidated. Very sheepishly, he says, "White, sir!"

"No, you're a yellow belt," says Hormoz mockingly.

He then turns around, and looking at the audience, he says, "I'm trying to teach these young men and women to always be prepared for unexpected interruptions in life."

Another group of kids who are older begin to appear from behind the back room. As they march in, Hormoz walks up to one of them and acts as if he is going to hit the kid. The poor kid has a frightened look on his face and cowers away. I can't believe what I'm looking at.

"I'm just trying to break your concentration by messing with your brain. You always have to be prepared for unexpected interruptions of life," says the man.

By now I'm pretty upset with the way the guy's treating these little kids. But what comes next is what really bothers me.

After mocking the students, Hormoz turns around, looks at my friend Rick, and very condescendingly asks, "Rick, what have you been teaching these kids?" I look at Rick and can tell he is quite embarrassed by the comment.

That does it. The man comes under my friend's roof as his guest in his studio and shames him in front of his students and their parents. Hormoz needs to be taught a lesson.

As he is running his mouth, from the back of the studio, I jump up and scream, "EXCUSE ME!" He literally jumps up. The whole place goes into a deadly hush. Everyone turns around and looks at me with much anticipation.

"What?" he asks.

"Nothing! Just messing with your mind trying to break YOUR concentration because you have to be prepared for unexpected interruptions in life." I sit down.

The place erupts in laughter. The parents had all felt the way I had but didn't know how to deal with the situation.

Looking at me, Hormoz raises his fist and says, "I'd like to break YOUR concentration." I'm so glad he's not serious. He can break a lot more than just my concentration.

After the meeting is over, Rick walks up to me and says, "Thank you for not letting me be embarrassed any further. I don't know what got into Hormoz today."

"Rick, that's what friends do for each other—protect one another's honor."

As we're talking in the driveway, Hormoz pulls up in his SUV with his girlfriend next to him. Rick introduces me to him and says, "This is the Iranian Christian I told you about." He seems to be a very nice man. We exchange a few words and say our good byes.

58

Soon after graduating from college, Karen got a **full-time job with Los Angeles County**. I became a full-time student working on my engineering degree. Karen literally worked her way through *my* schooling.

In those days it wasn't uncommon for Iranian men to marry American women for immigration reasons—as soon as their status was permanent, they'd divorce their wives. That used to infuriate me to a point that I refused to apply for my residency till two years after being married. I wanted to prove a point to the whole world—I didn't marry Karen for a "Green Card." However, that came with a price. For the two years I attended Cal State University in LA, we paid "out-of-state" tuition because I was considered a foreign student. I eventually got my degree in civil engineering.

Often when I'm speaking to an audience, looking very serious, I tell them, "Just so you know how much Christ changed my life and what a different person He made me become, through the power of the Holy Spirit, I was able to cram four years of college into *eight years.*"

Including high school, after twelve years of suffering and hard work, I now possessed a piece of paper, my diploma, which was magically supposed to bring me honor. I was no longer Aghayeh Afshar (Mr. Afshar), but Aghayeh Mohandess (Mr. Engineer). Six months later and after much prayer, I got a job with the LA County Flood Control. That was one of the greatest days of my life.

59

Very prophetically someone once told me, "All things will come to you late in life." Karen and I had agreed on starting a family as soon as I got a job. Two years into our marriage, she became a full-time housewife. Little did we know it was going to take us eight years before we could have our first child.

Karen was an infertility patient, and it took the doctors almost seven years to figure out what the problem was. At the time we were attending a church where the pastor and his wife's goal was to have ten children. Almost every nine months our pastor's wife was pregnant with a new baby.

Having to be happy for the couple wasn't easy. No, we weren't resentful; just having a hard time sharing in their joy, wondering why the same God who so easily granted Linda and Rich one baby after another was withholding the same blessing from us. After all, if he wasn't going to give us a child, why did he give us the desire for a family?

Of the two of us Karen, understandably, had the hardest time coping with the issue. Often, waking up in the middle of the night, I'd find her fully prostrated on the living room floor, crying out to God.

When answers to our prayers are delayed, we begin to wonder why God is withholding the answer. Maybe there's something in our lives that displeases him, maybe he wants to teach us something, maybe we need to pray harder, or maybe we lack sufficient faith.

That could very well be so, but it is hard to swallow that line of thinking when you see a 13-year-old get pregnant after having sex for the first time in the back of her 16-year-old boyfriend's car. If any act would be displeasing to God, it'd be what took place in the back of that car. Didn't they need to learn their lessons before two babies had one of their own? Especially when they didn't even pray or manifest any faith in making the baby?

I do realize these things today, but 30 years ago all I knew was what my mentors taught me—live righteously, and God will reward you. So, we prayed, fasted, sought God's face, and manifested faith.

One day I asked Karen what she'd do if she found out she was pregnant.

She said, "I'd start sewing baby clothes."

"Then, start sewing," I replied. And that she did. Thirty years later we still have the little bunnies she sewed in anticipation of having children, which I like to call an act of faith.

Eventually it was discovered that, due to scar tissue, Karen's fallopian tubes were blocked. To remove the scar tissue, Karen required two major surgeries. Soon after the second operation we had our first child, Todd Samuil, on February 1, 1982.

After reading the above story, some, who are in the same predicament as we were, might decide to use our act of faith as a formula. They might think, "*If it worked for the Afshars, it must work for us, so let's start sewing baby clothes.*" In all the years of following Christ, if I've learned anything, it's that God doesn't fit into any particular formula. Just because something works for me, there is no guarantee that it will for someone else. Is it possible that our act of faith had nothing to do with Karen getting pregnant? Is it possible that if we hadn't been standing in faith, Karen might have gone to her gynecologist much sooner?

It's a year after becoming a Christian. I'm standing in the middle of Pepperdine College campus where there's a fountain dedicated to Mr. Pepperdine's daughter. I decide I'm going to walk on water. After staring at the shallow pool for quite a while, I take my shoes and socks off and once again spend a few more minutes contemplating what I'm about to do—walk on water. I feel that if Jesus did it, I can do it too.[1] I remember reading in the New Testament *where he said that everything he did I can do also.[2] However, I eventually change my mind and decide against walking on water.*

Years later I'm sharing the story with a friend when he says, "Do you know why you didn't walk on water?"

"No, you tell me," I demand.

"Because you had no faith."

"But, I even took my shoes and socks off."

"Exactly! If you had any faith, you wouldn't have taken your shoes and socks off."

60

e named our son Todd because we wanted a name that both Iranians and Americans could pronounce. I wasn't about to put our child through my experience. He would not have to constantly correct how people pronounced his name or accommodate others to a point where he eventually was forced to shorten his name to something more easily pronounced.

Todd's middle name, Samuil, is the Persian form of Samuel, which in Hebrew means "heard of God." We felt, after years of prayer, God had finally heard us.

A year after Todd was born, Karen was pregnant again; but during the first trimester, she miscarried. It took us another three years before we had Megan Haleh. I loved the name Megan, which was taken from a blind character on a few episodes of the TV show *Rockford Files* with James Garner. Again, we chose the simple spelling of the name. My mother chose the Persian name Haleh, which means halo. Although we wanted at least four children, by the time Megan arrived, Karen and I were in our mid-30s, and with Karen experiencing a few illnesses, we knew having another child would be difficult.

We're in the middle of one of our annual Fellowship of Iranian Christians' summer conferences. Because of its novelty, it's quite popular. There are many Iranian believers who, for many years, thought they were the only Iranians from a

Muslim background to have become Christians. They're now excited to know they're not alone. There are several American missionaries who had spent years in serving Iran; they are now delighted to be around those for whom they'd prayed for so many years. We've been putting these conferences together since 1979.

Even though I put the conference together, due to my lack of organizational skills, Karen's in charge of running the whole thing. She's pregnant with our second child and taking care of Todd, who's only a year old. The place is like a zoo. There are so many last minute details that I've completely missed, which now have become Karen's responsibility.

Taking the afternoon off to visit my aunt and uncle who live in the area, it seems the stress level can't be any higher, when Karen informs me that she's bleeding. At first, hoping for the best, I try to ignore it; but the bleeding gets worse and worse. By now Karen is quite pale; but nobody else knows how to run the conference, so she has to continue. Towards the end of the conference, we rush her to an emergency hospital in Paso Robles. They can't do much for her, so we drive back to the conference ground. The next day, after we've made sure everything is accounted for and the conference center signs off on us, we head home, all the way praying that God would save the baby.

A few hours after we get home, Karen loses our second child. I retrieve the fetus before running Karen to ER. As I hold the fetus in my hand, realizing what I'd just put Karen through and trying to understand the pain my wife must be experiencing both physically and emotionally, I say to myself, "No ministry in the world is worth this." I wish I'd listen to myself.

61

Todd's quite articulate and has a gentle spirit. Karen and I joke about how no sooner did he exit his mother's womb, than he looked at both of us and said, "Good morning, mom and dad! I wonder what's for breakfast."

When he was only two and a half, Todd had a hernia operation, which required him to spend the night at the hospital. I spent the night with him, sleeping on the folding bed the hospital provided for me.

The next morning, when the nurse came to check on him, she asked Todd a question he didn't understand.

"Do you want to peepee?"

With a confused look on his face, Todd looked at her and then me.

"Do you want to weewee?" asked the nurse again.

Another puzzled look!

That's when I piped in, "Why don't you use the proper word?"

"Do you want to urinate?"

"Yes, please!" said Todd.

Rather apologetic, the nurse said, "I'm very sorry, but I've never seen a two year old who knows what 'urinate' means."

Just a few days later as he put a spoonful of oatmeal in his mouth, out of the blue, he uttered the words that brought tears to his mom and dad's eyes, "Jesus is in my heart."

However, our tears of joy turned into laughter when he swallowed the contents of his mouth and declared, "And now, he has oatmeal all over his face." He believed Jesus literally lived inside of him.

I am sitting behind the chain link fence watching Todd play on the playground at kindergarten. He's only five. The gentle spirit he's been blessed with prevents him from being a bully, even though he is taller than all his classmates. He'll eventually be 6'4".

He's playing tag with Jack, who doesn't like being tagged and begins to hit Todd. To end the confrontation, with the kid on his heels, Todd runs and sits next to the playground teacher who is Jack's grandmother, hoping to stop the beating without telling on the kid. Jack starts punching Todd, and the grandmother is not about to intercede.

Todd doesn't mind walking away from a confrontation, but he doesn't like to be cornered. As the kid raises his hand to hit him, Todd punches him out. One good hit and the kid is on the ground. That yanks the grandma out of her stupor, and she scolds Todd for hitting her grandchild. And that's when I step in pointing out who started the fight.

I'm so proud of my son. He's done all he can to stay away from trouble, but when trouble comes looking for him, he meets it head on and takes care of business.

62

It was the winter of 1978. I was working on my engineering master's degree at CSULA. A few weeks earlier, quite by accident, I'd run into another Iranian believer from Muslim background. He, like me, had become a follower of Christ in the U.S. After getting to know each other a bit and thinking that we must be the only Iranians from a Muslim background to become Christians, along with our American wives, we decided to start meeting regularly for Bible studies. Our plan was to eventually translate the Bible into Farsi. We had no idea that had been accomplished at least a good hundred years earlier.

It was soon after we began our meetings that the political unrest in Iran began to foment. The Islamic revolution was about to raise its ugly head, which caused a mass exodus of Iranian Christians from that land. In a short period, our small four-people meetings began to grow.

With the Islamic revolution, and especially the American Embassy hostage taking of 1979, came a deep interest in Muslim evangelism among the American churches. Suddenly American Christians wanted to know more about Islam, and people of my background became novelties. I was invited to speak at churches, and I offered my very limited knowledge on how to share our faith with Iranians. I realized people liked to listen to what I had to say and also laughed at my jokes. I'd finally found my niche in life—sharing with an audience the greatest story ever told, mixed with humor.

I'm supposed to meet Karen at a theater to catch a movie after work. She's waiting for me in line. It's day 65 of the hostage taking. Over two months ago some Iranian students broke into the American embassy in Tehran and took the employees hostage. Since then America's been consumed by the incident. Everyday one of the major TV news media reporters starts the world news by saying something like, "Day 65, America held hostage."

As I walk towards her, passing a long line of people waiting to get in, all of a sudden, for the first time in all the years I've been here, I feel like an outsider. People are looking at me differently. I probably look like one of the thousands of Iranians they see on the streets of Tehran every night on TV news shouting, "Death to America."

As the number of days into hostage taking gets longer and longer, completely aware of an average American's frustration with Iranians, I keep a low profile and jokingly tell everyone that I've changed my name to Pepe Rodriguez. I hear of some Iranian students getting beat up in other states, but they're the ones who'd marched around their schools in support of the hostage takers. I'm not naïve. I know there are racist Americans; but even through the hostage taking, I'm not experiencing any of the racism.

63

"**Y**ou're a bigot!" said the lady as we were walking to the school's cafeteria. Shelly was the dean's secretary and a good friend. What prompted her to call me a bigot was my reaction to her dating an Arab. She had just told me that she had dropped her Iranian boyfriend to date an Arab. My reply, albeit jokingly, was, "At least he is not an Iranian," which really ticked her off.

That day, on my way home, I had another one of those epiphanies. "Shahrokh, you are a bigot," I said to myself. "If you weren't, you wouldn't treat the Iranians around you like second-class citizens." Ever since I'd come to America, I'd decided not to have anything to do with Iranians. I felt I was better than they were. But, looking back, much of that was nothing but a "defense mechanism." I was ashamed of hanging out with Iranians because I would have to explain why I was such a failure.

That evening I announced to Karen, "I'm not going to continue with my master's degree, so I can focus on sharing the gospel with Iranians." That simple act of confrontation by Shelly led to establishing the first Iranian Christian organization in the United States—The Fellowship of Iranian Christians—something that Karen and I, along with a handful of Iranian Christians fresh out of Iran, started in 1978.

As I said earlier, I met Christ in English. The Christianity I knew was an American one. I didn't know it in Farsi when I lived in Iran, let alone, nine years after being in the U.S. speaking nothing but English.

I couldn't explain some of the most fundamental articles of my newfound faith in my mother tongue because I didn't have the vocabulary for it. I had to learn a whole new language, the Farsi "Christianese."

One of my newly found Iranian friends, Allahyar, gave me a cassette recording of a message by Rev. Hike Hosevpian, the foremost preacher in Iran. For several weeks I had my invited guests sit around a tape recorder and listen to the message in our living room. After that I transcribed the whole message word by word, memorized it, and taught it. Nothing was going to stop me from sharing the gospel with my own people in our own language.

Several years later I had the privilege of meeting Hike. Sometime in the early '90s he became one of the first Christian martyrs at the hands of the Islamic Republic of Iran.

Joel's a dear friend and a great hero of faith. He's been a missionary in Iran for many years and oversaw an orphanage there. Joel prides himself in being able to speak fluent Farsi; but like most Westerners, there are certain sounds he can't pronounce—sounds like "kh" or "gh."

On this particular Sunday at a church in Iran, he's preaching on "the power of the blood of Christ." In Farsi, the word for blood is "khoon," but Joel pronounces it "koon." So, for an hour he's preaching not on the power of the "blood" of Christ, but the power of the "koon" or "rear-end" of Christ.

64

Unlike Todd, Megan didn't say anything intelligible until she was over two years old. I still call her Lala-face because for those first two years, all she could say was, "lalalalalala." We often had to ask Todd to translate what his sister was saying, but even he didn't know. I encouraged her baby talk, so Megan wouldn't grow up as fast as Todd did. She stayed a child a bit longer. But she was much more adventurous and mischievous than her brother.

Where as our son is over 6'4", Megan is only 5'1"; yet, athletically, she's always been much more involved than her brother. She learned how to ride her bike before her brother. Megan not only learned how to swim early in life, but at high school she made it all the way to the city finals swimming the 100-meter butterfly event, her dad's event.

Both of our children are extremely smart, intelligent, and driven. Academically, Megan is like her mom. She graduated Summa Cum Laude from UCLA, and currently she's working on her doctorate. However, what I appreciate the most in both our children is their spiritual qualities. They both love God.

Megan's only 11. Her best friend, the girl down the street from us, has invited her to go to Disneyland for two days. They're going to spend the night in the Disneyland Hotel. Karen and I are both against it because we have never met the absent mother who has had a history of mental illness. We try to explain our deep concern, but DISNEYLAND FOR 2 Days! Boy, is Megan mad.

After she spends a good while arguing with me, begging, crying, and screaming, I send her to her room. I'm watching a football game and paying no attention to what she's doing in her room. I hear some occasional thuds of things hitting the floor, but I'm not about to leave my game. I love football.

I don't know how long has passed, but I notice Megan standing across from me looking at me. She's patiently waiting for the game to go into a commercial. As soon as there's a break, she walks up, puts her arms around me, tells me how much she loves me, and apologizes for her behavior. I'm stunned. We're talking about two days at Disneyland and a night at the Disneyland Hotel. What happened? Why am I so easily off the hook? I wonder if she's set her room on fire! She's quite capable of doing that, mind you.

"Dad," she begins, "when you sent me to my room, I was so angry with you, I decided to mess up my room. I first threw my stuff off the bed and then went for my books on the bookshelf. I started with the two bottom rows first. Among the books I threw on the floor, there were two Bibles. One of them landed on its spine and opened up to where it talks about God's love for us. I was immediately reminded of

God's love for me and his forgiveness for me, and suddenly all my emotions changed. I went from (she makes an angry look) to this (her happy face)."

She spends the next hour laying next me, hugging me as I continue to watch my game.

65

I **was in my seventh year working as an engineer,** which by now had become shear hell. I'd thought if I only prayed and worked hard at it, I'd eventually think and act like an engineer. After all, Saint Paul says, "I can do all things through Christ who strengthens me."[1] If it worked for Paul, it should work for me. All I needed was more faith and more prayer; but by then it was quite clear that either I didn't have enough faith or wasn't praying hard enough. There are more than a few holes in the above theological conclusion.

First, Paul is talking about himself. He claims that *he* can do all things through Christ. He isn't talking about me wanting to be an engineer. Next, within the context, all he's talking about is learning how to be content in life through Christ.[2] To take the above passage to such an unrealistic conclusion is much like the motivational speaker who tells a bunch of high school kids, "You can do whatever you put your mind to it." They both are bogus claims. I can neither do *all* things through Christ nor do *anything* I put my mind to. We all have our limitations within which God has created us, and there's nothing we can do about it but to be content and accept them.

I used to drive to work crying, knowing the project I'd turned in to my boss the day before would be full of red marks and pretty much rejected. I always felt ashamed in that office, knowing some of my colleagues made fun of me behind my back.

By now we had two kids and had just purchased an 850-square-foot, two-bedroom house. During the day I was Mr. Engineer, and in the evenings I ran three Iranian house churches in separate parts of the greater Los Angeles area. Iranians were becoming followers of Christ and needed training in their newfound faith.

This particular cold, dark, and depressing day, as I drove my '69 VW Bug, I began my usual conversation with God.

"***Lord!***" I had to scream very loud to make sure God could hear me over the noise of my beat-up car. "Why don't you make me a better engineer?" "Don't you see how your son is suffering?" "I thought you promised that I can do all things... Then what is going on?"

As usual, I didn't expect any answers. I was just venting. But this day was different.

"Son, whoever asked you to be an engineer?" I heard a voice ask. I recognized the voice. It was the same one that many years ago had asked, "Don't you think the man who walked on water can also take care of your problems?" Once again I'm in an "aha!" zone.

It makes me chuckle when I hear Christians tell me they live purely by the Word of God—as if something like that is even possible. We all look at the Bible through our own lenses developed by culture, upbringing, society, age, gender, and so on. No human can look at the Bible without any bias. Only God knows "*The* Reality." As fallen humans, we all make our own realities.

In my case, being raised in a shame-based culture, I was under the assumption that God thought like an Iranian—no college engineering degree, no respect.

That morning, once again, in a few short moments, my whole life changed. An overwhelming peace engulfed me. After years of struggles, I was given the freedom and permission to admit that I wasn't created to be an engineer and to not feel ashamed. I'm a storyteller. That's what God's made me for. By the time I got to my office I knew what I was supposed to do—quit my day job.

66

It's one thing to think you've heard from God, but it's another to convince others of it. I've seen too many Christians who've left a good-paying job to enter into so called "full-time ministry" without much concern for their wives and children. I believe there are times for taking leaps of faith. However, I also believe that he who asks you to take such leaps also gives you the faith and the intellect to prepare to do so. Now, I hated my engineering job with a passion, but I also had a family to support. I had to make sure I'd heard from God, and the best person to turn to was Karen.

It took me a few days before I shared my experience with my wife. For years Karen had watched my struggles, pain, and heartaches of wanting to be an engineer. She knew I wasn't trying to shun my responsibilities in pursuit of something more exciting to fulfill a personal void in my life. But Karen's always been the sensible and practical balance in our marriage. She knew we weren't ready to take the jump yet, and I agreed with her. So, we waited.

It took us another three years; but in 1987, after 10 years of being an engineer, I finally left my day job to do my night job full time—pastoring a small Iranian church. By then the Fellowship of Iranian Christians had been in existence for ten years as a group of small house churches.

A year later we founded "Nousazan" or the "Repairers," a Farsi-speaking church. I came up with the name while reading Isaiah 58:12. However, in English it was called The Iranian Church on the Way, named after the English-speaking church where we were meeting. I had to take a big pay cut, which eventually forced Karen to go back to working outside the house; but we both knew that was where we were supposed to be.

The church consisted of Iranian MBBs (Muslim-background believers) and Messianic Jews (Iranian Jews who believed Jesus to be the promised Jewish Messiah). It was one of a kind, extremely unique and diverse. I had no training in pastoring a church, but in those days my Pentecostal mentors looked down on any formal biblical training. Their attitude towards education and training was very much like the Mexican bandit's feeling towards badges in the movie *Blazing Saddle*: "Education? We don't need no stinking education." Once again, I had to rely on my dad's style of training—jump in first and then figure out how to stay afloat.

67

et's suppose I come to your house for dinner tonight. I'm sitting across from you. You need salt, and the saltshaker is in front of me. What would you do? As an American, you'll simply ask, "Would you please pass the salt?" If I were to ask you why you did it that way, your reply would be, "Because it is polite!"

Who told you that is polite?

"My mom," your answer might be.

Who did your mom learn that from? Probably her mother and her mother from her mother and so on. We have no idea when and where that custom began; but as far as you're concerned, to say "Please pass the salt" at the dinner table is proper etiquette.

I personally believe it started several hundred years ago when a little boy was crawling on the dinner table reaching for something. It annoyed his mother, so she smacked him alongside the head and said, "From now on and in this house, if you need something at the dinner table, you'll ask for it."

A couple of the neighborhood kids who were there heard the conversation, ran home, and told their parents. The parents exclaimed with glee, "What a novel idea! From now on, we will do the same at our homes, too." Before you know it, the city, then the county, the state, and eventually the whole nation decided to follow that rule as accepted etiquette. By the way, that is how most cultures start.

Now, let's reverse the situation. It is you who comes to my house for dinner. We are sitting across from each other. Now I need salt, and the saltshaker is in front of you. I will never ask you to pass the saltshaker. However, I will reach over and, while risking putting my sleeve in your soup, I pick up the saltshaker. Do you know why? Because my mother told me, "Shahrokh, to interrupt your guest while he is eating is not polite. If you need something, you get it yourself." My Iranian table etiquette is a world apart from yours.

It's been almost 42 years since the day I set foot in the United States of America. In all these years, I've struggled to create a reasonable balance between my Iranian culture and the American culture. When I sit at the dinner table and need the salt, I spent a good 10 to 15 minutes struggling with myself asking, "Should I reach? Or should I ask?" And, eventually I say to myself, "Screw it! Who needs salt? It's not good for you anyway."

I know I represent many displaced people who often struggle to reconcile two cultures they are faced with. Having come from a shame-based culture into one based on guilt, I have had to think creatively to produce a third culture. In my case, the glue that keeps this third culture together is the grace of God.

A man who's familiar with only one culture can't be held responsible for not knowing how to behave in a different one, but not in my case. I can't afford to make a mistake in either culture because I'm expected to know better.

I wrote this book for several reasons, but maybe the most important one is an attempt to offer hope to many, who, just like me, are facing a tremendous everyday challenge of reconciling cultures together. There is hope with God's grace.

Epilogue

Originally, I had chosen a different title for my book since it dealt with my Christian years. The farther I got into it, however, I realized that to justify that title, I needed to give my readers several hundred pages of introduction so they could understand where I was coming from. Being a great fan of short books, I decided to change the title in exchange for a shorter book with the hope that my next book, *With God, The First One is Always Free,* would start where this one ended.

Notes

Chapter 2

    1. Kenneth Scott Latourette, *History of Christianity,* vol. 1 (Peabody, MA: 1975), 77.

Chapter 32

    1. Philippians 4:13 (New King James Version).

Chapter 39

    1. 1 Corinthians 6:9–10 (NKJV).

Chapter 45

    1. John 9:24–25 (The Message Bible).

    2. Ibid., John 20:25.

    3. Ibid., vv. 27–28.

Chapter 46

    1. Philippians 4:6–7 (The Message).

Chapter 47

    1. See Galatians 3:6–9.

    2. See Psalm 17:8.

    3. See Acts 2:1–12.

Chapter 50

    1. See Mark 12:30.

Chapter 53

    1. See John 21:25.

Chapter 59

1. See Matthew 14:25–30.
2. See John 14:12.

Chapter 64

1. Philippians 4:13 (NKJV).
2. See Philippians 4:12.